THE CELTIC TAROT

THE
CELTIC
TAROT

HELENA PATERSON

Illustrated by
Courtney Davis

Aquarian/Thorsons
An Imprint of HarperCollins*Publishers*

The Aquarian Press
An Imprint of HarperCollins*Publishers*
77–85 Fulham Palace Road,
Hammersmith, London W6 8JB

Published by The Aquarian Press 1990
5   7   9   10   8   6   4

A catalogue record for this book
is available from the British Library

ISBN 0 85030 919 0

Typeset by Harper Phototypesetters Limited,
Northampton, England
Printed in Great Britain by
Woolnough Bookbinding Limited,
Irtlingborough, Northamptonshire

DEDICATION

To my mother, a lady of Faery blood
and infinite vitality.

Contents

Acknowledgements

The creative genius of Courtney Davis inspired the writing of this book and I thank him most sincerely. The support and understanding of my husband John made this challenge less daunting. Thanks are also due to Mary Bennett, who edited the book with astute comment and insight, to George and Eileen Benton-Smith and Jane Osborne-Fellows — special thanks for their encouragement and for having provided such useful reference books. A further appreciation is expressed to Jeremy Gilbert for giving me the opportunity to write this book.

Introduction

THE ORIGINAL CONCEPT
OF THE TAROT

The origins of the Tarot are vague and obscure. Tarot symbols have been linked to ancient Egyptian hieroglyphics found in temples and on the tombs of the Pharaohs. The very meaning of the word 'hieroglyph' is a picture or symbol representing a concept or sound that is difficult to read or decipher. It invites the question: did the ancient Egyptians perfect the symbolic language of hieroglyphics in order to conceal a message? Mystics and occultists believe that they did, and regard the hieroglyphs as symbols of higher knowledge and wisdom. Such wisdom, however, retains a mystical aura and confounds the believer and critic alike.

According to the occultists, this mystical concept of hidden wisdom, having germinated on the banks of the Nile, eventually propagated the Western cultures of Europe, via Greece, where it took root in the fertile minds of great scholars and artists, thus promoting a sense of spiritual and intellectual power. The first Tarot cards containing this mystical seed appeared in the Middle Ages, but they remained an incomplete set of symbols used mostly for fortune-telling, which rather denigrated their original concept.

Several centuries later, the French scholar Court de Gebelin began to examine the Tarot with more insight. In 1773 he published the first part of a massive work entitled

Le Monde Primitif in which he expressed a tentative opinion on the Tarot. He suggested that the Tarot was part of an ancient Egyptian book of magic. It not only attracted a renewed interest in the Tarot, but drew public attention to Egyptian mysticism. When the Rosetta Stone was found in 1799 it provided the key to deciphering the hiero-glyphics and aroused further speculation among the esoterics.

During the middle of the nineteenth century another Frenchman, Alphonse Louis Constant, began to decipher the Tarot. He was a philosopher and artist who studied the occult. Under the pseudonym of Eliphas Levi, he wrote a complete treatise on *Magic*, setting down the foundation of the Major Arcana cards. But he concealed their correct numerical sequence in order to preserve their sacred truth. A number of Tarot decks appeared in print, but the earlier Marseilles Tarot remains one of the classics of the Tarot. Its symbolism is the purest, retaining the original concept of the Tarot from the Middle Ages.

By the late nineteenth century, various occult societies in England began publishing their own concepts of the Tarot. The Golden Dawn Tarot and Aleister Crowley's Thoth Tarot Deck were eagerly acclaimed in esoteric circles. Later, A. E. Waite in 1910 presented his version known as the Rider-Waite deck. Thanks to the powerful drawings of the artist, Pamela Coleman-Smith, it became the most successful and well-known Tarot. The correct numerical sequence is still open to conjecture, but the Tarot had evolved into a complete system of symbolism.

Esoterics believe the Tarot symbols form the un-conscious link between the dual nature of man and his Creator — a pictorial album with each card represent-ing an intimate aspect of that relationship. The Tarot has also been linked with the Qabalist Tree of Life, a comple-mentary system of symbolism along with astrology and alchemy. Each system is regarded as a complete emana-tion or divine source of creative evolution. The Qabalist

Tree is the root source and aligned to the element of Earth; alchemy, the predecessor of chemistry, is the spiritual element of Fire; astrology formed the basis of ancient astronomy, the element of Air; the Tarot is the imagery of the soul, the element of Water.

In the Tarot, the elements symbolize the four-dimensional qualities of character in the abstract sense, but the essence of the Tarot remains the Water element of imagery. It is a mirror which can reflect great depths of self-realization or false illusion. This may explain some of the controversy surrounding the Tarot. The interpretation must be clearly defined and understood. The reader should have a working knowledge of the symbolism of each card, which will increase with practice.

THE CELTIC TAROT

There is at present an immense interest in the search for esoteric knowledge as people around the world begin to revise their ideologies and role in the universe. The spiritual climate appears to correspond with the changing meteorological conditions.

The Celts had identified the changing seasons with the spiritual cycle of man, and it added a dimension of consciousness to their lives which raised their perception of the natural and supernatural world. They had a Western tradition of esoteric knowledge that has been sadly ignored and neglected. The Arthurian legends of the Celts are more generally known. The fabulous quest for the Holy Grail is written about with increasing enthusiasm and speculation. It contains a wealth of mystical wisdom and reveals the Celts' spiritual nature.

The Celtic Tarot has been devised in order to re-establish a lost legacy of Celtic art and mythology within the ancient wisdom of the Tarot. Courtney Davis, the artist who created the Celtic Tarot, was inspired by the revival of Celtic thought and vision. His artistry has reconstructed the Tarot symbols with classical style and symbolism. The imagery is rich and flamboyant, and spiritually powerful — a reflection of the Celtic character.

The spiral symbols represent eternal life, and the intricate knotwork spiritual growth. The key patterns are a continuation of spirals and form complex labyrinths. The design of the labyrinth represents the spiritual search for immortality, and has been found in ancient temples around the world. Celtic monks illustrated their manuscripts with these brilliant decorations and symbols, showing once again the evolutionary thread of spiritual consciousness.

In pre-Christian days, the Druids were the priests and prophets of the Celtic people. Their conception of death was remarkably similar to the Egyptians, who also believed in the immortality of the soul — a doctrine preached by Pythagoras and many pre-Christian light bearers. In the Druids' symbolic system, the four elements of the universe were the Four Spirits or Four Winds of God. The four elements represented two dual forces: Heaven and Earth (for Air and Earth), the Sun and Moon (for Fire and Water).

Druidic philosophy and religion provide an insight into the mystical nature of Man which is still relevant today. The element of mysticism surrounding the Tarot requires a careful balance and practical application. The Tarot is a powerful source of inner wisdom and the means of acquiring relevant information. The ability to foretell certain events is the divinatory aspect of the Tarot, but it must be tempered with prudence. It is not a parlour game designed to promote a sense of fatalism.

The Celtic Tarot Deck remains a traditional interpretation, with the Celtic artwork recalling the intricate energies and emotions of man.

A CELTIC PROFILE

The origin of the Celts is as vague and mysterious as that of the Tarot. They were initially a confederacy of seafaring tribes who appear to have originated from various islands in the Aegean Sea during the Bronze-Age civilization of Greece. Their language and art is closely aligned to the Cretan/Minoan period of Greek history: 3000-1100 BC. Some historians believe that it was the Syrian invasion of the Greek islands which displaced them. A more romantic but plausible theory identifies them with the remnants of the Trojan race. Whether escaping or seeking conquest, they began to move northwards in the middle to late Bronze Age, dispersing up the Danube and once again dividing eastwards through the Carpathian Mountains and westwards to Switzerland.

Another group took the Mediterranean route and sailed through the Straits of Gibraltar to Spain and ancient Gaul. Around 500 BC they conquered Spain from the Carthaginians and settled in large numbers in Spain and Gaul. A short period later they overcame the Etruscans in Northern Italy. A 'Golden Age of Celtia' commenced, and they became the greatest power in pagan Europe. They marched to Rome in the year 391 BC and sacked the city after annihilating the Roman Army. A century later they returned to Greece and sacked Delphi. Strangely enough, they remained on good terms with the Greeks and later forged an alliance with Alexander the Great against the Persians and Phoenicians.

The first proto-Celtic people to arrive by the sea route landed in Ireland and North Britain in 1472 BC. They were known to the Irish as the 'Tuatha de Danaan', reaching Ireland after first landing in Denmark. Two hundred years later, another Achaean invasion of tribes who came from Thrace (ancient country of Western Greece and Eastern Turkey) arrived in Ireland. After fierce opposition the new invaders were forced to move over to Northern Britain.

They were known as the Picts — the tattooed people who decorated their bodies for battle, in which their women also participated.

There were successive waves of people arriving in Britain between 2000-1500 BC. They were called the 'Beaker People' who came from Spain by way of Southern France and the Rhine. They appeared to have settled down peacefully with the ancient Stone-Age Briton. Their knowledge of metal-working and the custom of burying their dead had the hallmarks of the proto-Celt. They were perhaps the first arrivals of the overland Celt from Switzerland. From 1500-600 BC they developed the Bronze-Age culture and further integrated with the indigenous tribes.

The invading tribes of Goidelic people around 600 BC were migrants from the Baltic coast of Germany. They brought with them the 'Hallstadt' Iron-Age culture from central Europe. This knowledge of iron working originated somewhere in the Eastern Alpine area. Two acknowledged theories place it from up the Adriatic and across the Balkans; or, up the Adriatic and across southern Russia. The Goidelic people were certainly proto-Celtic. Their language, Gaelic, became one of the main Celtic tongues. Considering that they were forced to remain in the southeastern counties it was an extraordinary feat of conquest, which suggests another theory. They may very well have been the early Celts who had taken the Carpathian route having trekked across the Balkans to Germany. They did not in fact impose their own language, but found the descendants of their own race.

The last two successive waves of invaders were the Belgic people. From 400-300 BC and 50 BC-45 AD, they overran a greater part of Britain and Ireland. They were a mixture of Brythons and Teutons; their 'La Tène' Iron-Age culture was the continental Celtic hybrid. It took root and flourished, creating a true Celtic identity and race. There still remained tribal territories, however, and their language had two definite divisions: Goidelic or Gaelic became the language of Ireland, the Scottish Highlands and the Isle of Man; Brythonic or British became the language of Wales and the Cornish Celts, who had always maintained close ties with the Breton Gauls.

Their character and temperament has always been fiery and passionate, quick to take offence and yet chivalrous in victory. A warlike race, who fought better on horseback or as charioteers, their love of display was shown in their richly embroidered garments and ornate weapons. They were articulate, and passionately fond of music and the arts. Their physical appearance has been described as tall, fair, and aristocratic. Their women, who were considered extremely beautiful and more dangerous than the male, were known to participate in battle, especially if their men were losing ground. They feared no mortal being, but were fearful of ghosts and the Sidhe — the Faery people.

The religion of the Celts must have taken into account the imposing relics of the Megalithic people who first inhabited the British Isles. Druidism actually evolved with the Celtic conquest of Britain and Ireland. The Celts had found a people already steeped in magic and mysticism. The ancient chambered tombs or cromlechs were an extraordinary link with their own beliefs of immortality. Their religious development was the blending of several powerful deities or beliefs and conducted through magical rites. The Gallic Celts revered Dis, or Janus, the god of the Underworld, from whom they claimed descent. The Irish Celts were drawn to solar gods and their God of Light, Lugh, became the polarity to the powers of darkness.

As they began to integrate their religious beliefs, the Goddess aspect emerged with increasing status. The lunar goddess of all Celts was Arianrhod, the Lady of the Silver Wheel, but her mysterious cult remained one of the darker aspects of the Celtic religion. As the 'Morrigan' in Irish legends she was a Death-goddess who assumed the shape of a raven. Her triple aspect of Maiden-Mother-Hag is the female deity to Dis. The Celts had always followed a matrilineal system of kingship. Daughters could rule in their own right, and the sons of the king's sisters were the legal claimants to the throne.

The Celtic conception of death has been only briefly touched upon. Whilst their idea of immortality followed similar lines to the Greeks, and indeed all classical civilizations, their conception of death was altogether very different. The Greeks and Romans saw the Under-world of the Dead as a gloomy place of suffering, from which it was no easy task to escape or come back to life. The Celts regarded death with more optimism, and this was reflected by their fearless attitude in battle. They believed that they went immediately to a place of light and liberation — the Island of Youth — the son of their Sea-god Lir, Manannan, conducted them across the sea, where they became young again. They could then choose whether to come back or stay. Evil people were dealt with more severely and had to start again from the lowest form of animal life.

The Druids were a priestly caste, their knowledge of healing and medicine has been commented upon by numerous ancient Greek and Roman historians. Their twenty-year training was long and arduous. It was based on a bardic tradition and a knowledge of the sciences — alchemy and astronomy. When they finally put on the white robes of the Druid and the gold crescent collar, their authority was a formidable power.

Their Druidic philosophy and teachings evolved into a structure that played a very important part in the religious development of Western Europe. This teaching is found principally in two volumes of ancient Welsh literature entitled *Barddas*; it contains an esoteric doctrine which suggests a pre-Christian mystic philosophy.

There has been an unfortunate gap in the history of the Celts, which has rather displaced them, and they have been referred to as the 'Celtic Fringe' — a misnomer if there ever was one. They still represented the larger percentage of the population after the Anglo-Saxon invasions; whilst Scotland and Ireland had remained totally Celtic during the Roman and Saxon invasions. The Irish Celts continued to settle in equally large numbers in the Western regions of Britain for many centuries following the Saxon invasions. The British today refer to their Anglo-Saxon heritage when it would be more correct to speak of an Anglo-Celtic population and ethnology. It is the Celtic plus the Germanic elements which make up the British character. It is a unique fusion, a blend of passionate belief with the more pragmatic Teuton.

Using the cards

How to handle and use the cards is the first step to understanding the Tarot. Some people already conversant with the Tarot will have their own system and method. There is a tendency amongst 'professional' Tarot readers to engender a mystical aura by wrapping the cards in a silk scarf or by keeping them in a special box. This is a personal preference rather than a necessary requirement, but it is advisable to keep them safe and not leave them lying around. Before attempting any spreads, get to know the feel of the cards and concentrate on the pictorial images. This will ensure the first unconscious link with the more complex symbolism.

THE SIGNIFICATORS

There are a variety of spreads and methods for selecting cards. Whether you are doing them for yourself or another, the first step is to select a significator. This represents the questioner or querent. If you decide to place yourself as the querent, select a card accordingly. The Court cards are used as the significators because they represent the individual forces of character. There are, however, several traditional associations with the Court cards which can be confusing. For example, if the Queen of Coins is chosen to represent a dark-haired mature woman, bear in mind that this card is also associated with the element of Earth, and denotes a character who is very practical and reliable, which may not fit the woman at all. The easiest way to

select a significator is by using the querent's Zodiac sign.
The following astrological associations will tell you at a
glance which one to select:

Card	Type	Zodiac Sign
King of Wands	a mature man over forty	Aries, Leo, Sagittarius
Queen of Wands	a mature woman over forty	Aries, Leo, Sagittarius
Knight of Wands	a young man under forty	Aries, Leo, Sagittarius
Page of Wands	a youth or young girl	Aries, Leo, Sagittarius
King of Cups	a mature man over forty	Cancer, Scorpio, Pisces
Queen of Cups	a mature woman over forty	Cancer, Scorpio, Pisces
Knight of Cups	a young man under forty	Cancer, Scorpio, Pisces
Page of Cups	a youth or young girl	Cancer, Scorpio, Pisces
King of Swords	a mature man over forty	Gemini, Libra, Aquarius
Queen of Swords	a mature woman over forty	Gemini, Libra, Aquarius
Knight of Swords	a young man under forty	Gemini, Libra, Aquarius
Page of Swords	a youth or young girl	Gemini, Libra, Aquarius
King of Coins	a mature man over forty	Taurus, Virgo, Capricorn
Queen of Coins	a mature woman over forty	Taurus, Virgo, Capricorn
Knight of Coins	a young man under forty	Taurus, Virgo, Capricorn
Page of Coins	a youth or young girl	Taurus, Virgo, Capricorn

When you become more familiar with the cards, you will be able to select the significators intuitively, regardless of any astrological or traditional associations. Whilst the Court cards symbolize the personal qualities of character, some people are drawn to choosing a card which has a special significance. The Minor Arcana can be used thus, but the Major Arcana cards should not be used as significators. Their action is an external force which cannot be diverted into an internal situation without creating a distortion of imagery.

Having selected the significator, choosing the cards for the spread is an important consideration. There are once again several methods — a matter of personal choice rather than a set format. Some people spread all the cards out in a line across the table and select the number required for the spread. The use of a pendulum can provide a powerful guide if the querent is at all hesitant.

Another method which is highly recommended is first to separate the Major Arcana cards from the Minor cards. The querent will then shuffle and cut the cards back together three times. This allows the querent to sort out his or her own karmic pattern, a very personal and significant action. Having decided the spread, proceed to draw the number required off the top of the deck and lay all the cards face downwards. The person reading the spread should then turn up all the cards slowly and with quiet concentration. Each card provides a complete source of information relevant to the position in the spread. The whole spread, however, does reflect a much wider and indepth summary.

DIGNIFIED AND ILL-DIGNIFIED CARDS

The interpretation of the cards takes into account a system known as 'dignified' or 'ill-dignified'. Some people prefer to use reversed cards and deliberately shuffle them in. This is really a matter of personal choice again, but the method of interpretation used with the Celtic Tarot follows the system described above. The significance of the cards then depends entirely on the neighbouring cards.

A favourable or unfavourable card always remains true to its symbolism, but it can be displaced or held in check if the card drawn next to it has an opposite principle. The position of the cards clarifies this point. If a difficult card is drawn which represents a past situation and the following cards show a favourable outcome, it is reasonable to conclude that the negative influence has been dealt with. If the card is potently negative, e.g. the Ten of Swords, there will remain a residue of mental tension.

The Suit of Wands are largely optimistic cards, full of vigour and enterprise. The Suit of Cups are more vulnerable, full of hopes and dreams not fully realized. The Suit of Swords are the corrective measures, full of harsh realities and a need to communicate more openly. The Suit of Coins are concerned with more fundamental issues, full of materialistic attitudes and values.

Swords contain several cards which are ill-dignified influences when drawn next to any card in the deck, the most difficult being the Three, Five, Eight, Nine, and Ten. The interpretation of each card should again clarify this point. Practice, and learning the symbolism of the cards, is the key to understanding whether a card is dignified or ill-dignified. A simple rule is always to read the card as dignified, and then look very carefully at the neighbouring cards to assess their positive or negative qualities which are contained in the description of the card. It is not as straightforward as using reversed cards, but by being able to assess each card on its individual merit, the imagery of the Tarot flows more freely.

SPREADS

The Celtic Cross

The Celtic Cross is one of the most well known and useful spreads. It will provide a definite answer to questions and shows the past, present and future pattern of events. Having selected a significator, place it face upwards on the table. Shuffle and cut the deck three times. Draw the cards from the top and lay face downwards. Follow the correct numerical order and design of the spread as shown (see Fig 1, p.26). Turn up the cards. The interpretation of the positions is as follows:

1 The card placed over the significator shows the prevailing influence. It also represents the nature of the querent.
2 This card shows the opposing forces or matters which require a positive approach and rectification. Favourable cards will mean a surprise victory. This card is placed across the first card, but is always read as an upright or dignified card.
3 This card represents the ideal solution, or what will actually be achieved — good or bad.
4 This card is the heart of the matter and represents both past and present influences.
5 This card is a past and passing influence which no longer needs to be taken into account.
6 This card shows future influences which will occur shortly, and remain in place for the coming year.
7 This card represents the position and attitude of the querent, how he or she is in fact responding to the situation.
8 This card shows the home and environment of the querent, also family influence and matters of a domestic nature.

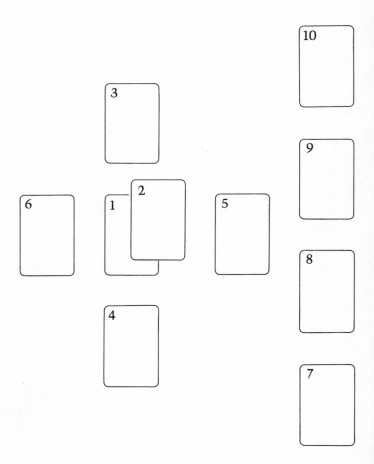

Fig. 1   The Celtic Cross Spread

9   This card will pick up the hopes and fears of the querent, which may be contrary to the question asked.
10 This is the most important card of the spread and requires special attention and focus. It shows the final outcome and can be used as a follow-on card in a second spread to clarify detail. Place this card over the significator and reshuffle and cut the deck, then proceed with the Celtic Cross spread.

The Alchemist's Spread

This is one of the oldest-known spreads and came into use towards the end of the Middle Ages in France. It is reputed to have been devised by Nostradamus, a physician and astrologer of extraordinary vision. His book of prophesies was written in peculiar verse to disguise the revelationary content. He was, after all, living in dangerous times when divination of any kind was considered subversive and evil by the Church. However, the patronage of Queen Catherine de Medici granted him a certain immunity and protection. The Alchemist's spread is a very potent one, which should only be drawn once. It contains the whole structure of man aligned with the universe; the macrocosm and microcosm unite in this spread — a six-pointed star.

First, place the significator in a central position and shuffle the cards accordingly. Place them face downwards in the correct numerical order and design (see Fig 2, p.28). Turn up the cards. The interpretation of the positions is as follows:

1   Past: representing the accumulated karma and all past life experience.
2   Present: representing everything which will be achieved in this life.

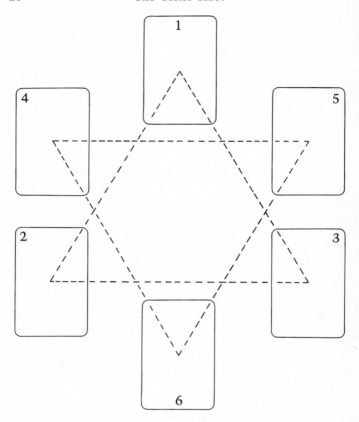

Fig. 2   The Alchemist's Spread

3   Future: representing the end of the matter, the final
    position on the Wheel of Life.
4   Shows the future influences which will occur —
    shortly.
5   Shows the future influences which will occur — over
    the next few years.

6   Shows the future influences which will occur —
     ultimately.

If this spread is drawn more than once it will start to
dissolve into what the querent desires and will not be a
true visionary guide.

The Druid's Star

This spread has been devised to complement the Celtic
Tarot. It is an original concept, using the four elements of
the Tarot. The first four cards represent the elements in a
Solar mode of action: direct, open, and positive. The last
four cards represent the elements in a Lunar action:
indirect, hidden, and passive. The design of the eight-
pointed star is linked to the eight sacred festivals of the
Druids. The festivals were the four fire festivals of the Sun,
and the four Lunar festivals of their Goddess. The dual
principle is a perfect balance of energies and the Tarot
symbols respond accordingly.

   This is not a divining spread for future reference, but it
will provide some indepth analysis on the character and
the present position in life and is a therefore a useful
spread for counselling. No significator is required for this
spread. The first card represents the querent.

   Shuffle and cut the cards three times. Use the cards
from the top and place them face downwards in the correct
numerical order and design (see Fig 3, p.30). Turn up the
first four cards, but leave the other four cards face
downwards. The interpretation of the positions is as
follows:

1   Represents the Fire element of character — the active
     and enterprising qualities. It shows what is relevant at
     the moment.

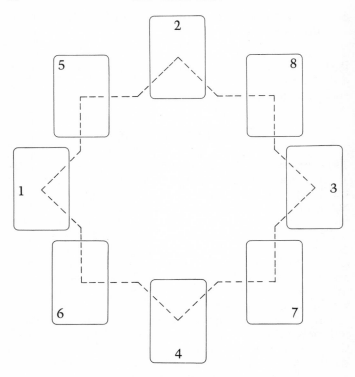

Fig. 3   The Druid's Star Spread

2   Represents the Water element of character — the
    emotive and expressive qualities. It shows hopes and
    dreams.
3   Represents the Air element of character — the in-
    tellectual and communicative qualities. It shows
    positive attitudes and approach to the situation.
4   Represents the Earth element of character — the
    materialistic and practical qualities. It shows
    requirements and the personal-value system.

Now turn up the four remaining cards. The interpretation of the positions is as follows:

5   This card is aligned to the first card: it shows any health problems and hidden weaknesses of character.
6   This card is aligned to the fourth card: it shows inherited traits of character — good or bad.
7   This card is aligned to the third card: it shows the dual nature and the type of partners who are compatible.
8   This card is aligned to the second card: it shows hidden fears and the level of emotion.

The Major Arcana

The Tarot consists of 78 cards and is divided into two integral parts. The Major Arcana has 22 cards and the Minor Arcana 56 cards. The Major Arcana represents a universal structure, the macrocosm. The Minor Arcana represents the human potential — the microcosm. The Major cards symbolize the archetypal images of mythology which represent an inherited memory or a mental picture of certain phases of evolution. Although each card has a defined principle, they are manifesting phases of evolution rather than fixed limitations.

The Celtic Tarot has re-created the archetypal images of the Celts to provide the Major Arcana with new impetus. The journey of The Fool has always represented the traditional cycle of spiritual initiation and rebirth; Celtic gods and Druidic mysticism evolved into a cosmology, a higher philosophy than religious dogma.

The Major Arcana cards have been referred to as the 'karmic pattern' of the individual soul which spans several centuries. They will recall important information and future progress of the querent on the greater Wheel of Life. If the spread contains several Major Arcana cards, it indicates a crucial period of learning and development. The symbolism of the Major Arcana is evocative and will create a personal imagery according to the individual karma, but it remains outside the control of the individual. The cards have been listed for quick reference with key words designed to convey their meaning.

Number	Card	Key Words to Interpretation
0	Fool	new cycles, ideals, vanity
1	Magician	integrity, subtle changes, illusion
2	High Priestess	hidden wisdom, spirituality
3	Empress	motherhood, refinement, idleness
4	Emperor	father figure, benefactor, obstacles
5	Hierophant	religion, servitude, obligations
6	Lovers	inspired love, partnerships, polarities
7	Chariot	compromise, vitality, past errors
8	Strength	justice, consolidating action, sexual motives
9	Hermit	humility, wisdom, austerity
10	Wheel	good fortune, optimism, sudden changes
11	Justice	adjustments, harmony, bigotry
12	Hanged Man	intuitive wisdom, personal sacrifices
13	Death	regeneration, critical changes, losses
14	Temperance	purification, moderation, waste
15	Devil	temptation, exposed vices
16	Tower	sudden disasters, opposition, purging action
17	Star	spiritual vision, birth, independence
18	Moon	imagination, hidden enemies, elusive forces
19	Sun	integration, contentment, achievement
20	Judgement	important decisions, crucial changes
21	World	realization, an evolutionary freedom

The Major Arcana cards are listed with reference to their Celtic archetype to provide a useful first impression and image.

Number	Card	Celtic Archetype
0	Fool	Great Fool, Dalua
1	Magician	Archdruid
2	High Priestess	Ceridwen, of the Lake of Tegid
3	Empress	Earth Goddess, Tailltiu
4	Emperor	King Arthur Pendragon
5	Hierophant	The Willow Tree
6	Lovers	Tristan and Iseult
7	Chariot	Cuchulain
8	Strength	Queen Macha
9	Hermit	Merlin
10	Wheel	The Morrigan
11	Justice	Queen Dana
12	Hanged Man	Sea-serpent
13	Death	Janus, God of the Underworld
14	Temperance	St Keyne, Celtic Saint
15	Devil	Cenchos, the Footless One
16	Tower	The Round Towers of the Culdees
17	Star	The Rowan Tree
18	Moon	Arianrhod, Lady of the Silver Wheel
19	Sun	Lugh, God of Light
20	Judgement	The Alder Tree
21	World	The Circle of Gwynvydd

The Fool

The Fool represents the beginning of a journey and is symbolized by the youthful figure of a young man dressed in green — a traditional colour of spring. He appears to be

intoxicated by the perfume of a white rose and oblivious to his sudden leap from a rocky precipice into space. But the element of Air, a symbol of the Spirit — an unconfined energy which permeates all things — controls his action. This is shown in the background, with the movement of Air delicately traced through the Celtic art of interlacing, rather than in precise shapes or solid form.

The Sun has already risen to its zenith and is slowly descending; a symbol of the beginning and end of a cycle, which is something of an enigma until the significance of The Fool begins to be understood. It has been called the most profound card in the Tarot and summarizes the soul's quest for wisdom and perfection.

The staff slung over his shoulder is tied with a small bundle. It represents all his worldly goods, which seem rather meagre. It is symbolic, however, of the impulsive nature rejecting the material life for something of more value. The surrounding mist symbolizes the mysterious element or nature of his quest, whilst the two dog-like animals simultaneously urge him onwards and pull him back from the dangerous vacuum now created. The hounds represent the positive and negative forces that operate in the earthly regions.

The Fool in the Celtic Tarot can be linked to the 'Great Fool' — Dalua — of the Celts. A fundamental belief in many ancient civilizations is the association of madness or fools with great wisdom. Fools and young children are inclined to speak the truth. They are also the mediums in the group or racial consciousness, unblemished by sin and surrounded by the light of the soul.

The card is also linked to the Spring festival — the first of February in the Celtic calendar — and represented by the Goddess Brigantia. She is the young maiden aspect of the Celtic Lunar Goddess. This particular aspect is part of the three cycles of spiritual growth: germination, re-growth, decay — but not death. The changes taking place are part of the eternal cycle of life and demonstrated in the number of The Fool — 0 — an element of addition which cannot be quantified.

This card actually deals with asking for advice. It represents an intention or an ambition in the early stages: shall I? or shan't I? If the querent draws this card it reflects his or her own uncertainty in the matter. A querent might be quite literally on the brink of making a disastrous move which could have considerable repercussions or find his or her decision is correct at the time, even if friends and family think the querent is being hasty and ill-advised.

Dignified It means trusting one's own judgement and going ahead, but with the making of plans, rather than a definite commitment. Generally it is not a good influence concerning money or financial investments. If this is clearly understood, a new cycle is indicated which provides real growth in a spiritual and intellectual sense.

Ill-dignified The querent might be stepping into the vacuum of apathy, extravagant gestures and the sheer folly of vanity. A form of fanaticism will exist which blinds the querent to truth or sane advice. All the human eccentricities surface creating chaos and confusion. One false step, in other words, and the querent might very well overturn his/her very existence.

The Fool is an undetermined force subject to the intentions and the ideals of the querent.

The Magician

This card represents the Universal Magician or Arch-druid, evoking an image of the universal energies with the Wand of Fire. Such energies are controlled by the powers attributed to Mercury or the Celtic Mugher — a planet traditionally associated with the card, symbolizing action in all forms and phases of life. The symbols shown within the Zodiac Wheel are the energies controlled by the six-pointed Star of David, a symbol of the evolved Man or Magus.

This is enforced by the horizontal figure of eight placed in the first point of the star, a symbol of infinity, which represents the closed circle of energy operating within the universe. The crossed sword and wand represent a balance of the elements — Air and Fire — a spiritual balance of life and death. Neither pierces the immortality of the soul, represented by the chalice or cup, a Water element of purity of vision.

Many ancient civilizations, including the Celts, believed that all life emanated from the element of Water. The Celts also believed the dead were conveyed in a boat by Manannan, son of their Sea-god Lir, to the Land of Youth. The boat, without oar or sail, was controlled by the thought of Manannan. He was man's spiritual guide, but he was also a master of tricks and illusions, the attributes linked to Mercury, the artful Messenger of the Gods. The chalice, placed within the circle of light, is the most potent symbol of love and unity with God. It was later identified in Arthurian legends with the Quest of the Holy Grail, a search for the very life force or blood of God.

The four Celtic figure-heads outside the Zodiac Wheel represent the positive and negative thoughts under the control of the querent. The top two are sea-horses, symbols of positive fire and water. The bottom two are symbols of a demon called Cenchos — 'The Footless' — a force of negative evil.

The robed figure of the Archdruid has a white inner

robe, symbolic of an Initiate of 'purity and vision'. The outer red robe, flecked with gold, is symbolic of positive thought. The golden pentacle around his neck shows man's own limitations — a magic symbol of Earth.

This card has great force and meaning; it reveals the changes taking place around the querent are sometimes difficult to understand, but are instigated by an inner desire to come to terms with a situation. Some kind of change is necessary, but the power of the energies evoked requires a steady nerve to assimilate the changes taking place within the very nature or character of the querent. The Magician has also been referred to as 'The Juggler' in some Tarot decks — a title which provides another image of events and actions being carefully staged to create an illusion.

Dignified It may appear at times that the querent is being manipulated in some strange way. The positive response is to rely on intuitive and meditative thought to determine the right course of action. The surrounding cards hold the answers as to why this is happening, or perhaps more important, who is responsible for this action.

Ill-dignified The querent is subject to self-deceit and illusions of a selfish nature. There may be an inclination to lie and cheat on others caught up in the current situation. The querent may also be the victim of lies and deceit, or inclined to hold on to material gains at the expense of others, and ultimately delay his or her own release from the great Zodiac Wheel of life.

Although the Magician is a neutral adviser or agent he is

above all testing the integrity of the soul and the actions of the querent.

The High Priestess

The High Priestess is standing between two pillars of Light and Darkness which represent the dual aspect of the Celtic Lunar Goddess. The Moon and the element of Water are associated with the role of the High Priestess, and in this aspect of the Goddess she was known to the Celts as 'Ceridwen of the Lake of Tegid'. The card is linked with initiation and enlightenment, the realm of mystery and magic.

Her robe of deepest blue is a traditional colour of both virginity and motherhood, which later became symbolic

of the Virgin Mary in the conversion of the Celts to Christianity. It was an easy transition to make, for they already believed that Ceridwen had given birth to the Sun through a mystical union with their Creator — Celi. Ceridwen had first created the Magic Cauldron of Inspiration, represented in the card as the energies of Earth held in the crescent Moon. It was also called the Sacred Cauldron, later to be associated with the Holy Grail as the Celts transplanted their ancient beliefs into the Christian concept of God.

She is holding in her hand the Seed of the Silver Star, the element of radiant or pure thought, a symbol of the highest initiation. After various initiations, the infant son who finally emerged on the twenty-second day of December was called 'Taliesen', 'the re-born' or 'the thrice-born into the outer world', corresponding very conveniently to Christmas Day, which represents Christ's own birth date. The golden disc behind her head is a symbol of the solar energies. The Sun, Moon, and Earth thus united form the Celtic Trinity of Father-Mother-Son. The Christian religion had evolved from a patri-archal culture and preferred to call it Father–Son–Holy Ghost.

The pillars of Light and Darkness are united through the arc over the golden disc by the energies of an earthly nature. The card also relates to the residue found in the Sacred Cauldron which contained the sins and pollutions of the novices. The initiation aspect of the High Priestess is being able to confront the darker elements of self; what transpires is the mysterious element of the card known only to the querent.

The card is a feminine force and relates to women generally. It will represent the querent if a woman, or the woman involved with the querent if a male. But the High Priestess symbolizes the spiritual nature of both men and women, therefore it has equal worth as a card for both. When this card is drawn it usually indicates that the querent is troubled by the future for a variety of reasons. There are changes in his or her life already taking place which may be causing some problems.

Dignified It shows great tenacity and wisdom in dealing with these problems. This might not appear obvious to others, but the querent is gathering strength quietly and with equal deliberation behind the scenes. The card also relates to the arcane arts and sciences, which may interest the querent as the means of learning at a particularly important stage of personal development.

Ill-dignified It shows a superficial knowledge and an immoral nature. It can invoke a passion rather than an ideal state of consciousness. The neighbouring cards must therefore be carefully considered before interpreting this card fully.

The High Priestess is a source of inspiration and represents the truth behind both light and darkness.

The Empress

The figure of the Empress rising from the blue-green mist was identified with Venus or Aphrodite who, according to the ancient Greeks, sprang from the sea and as she stepped ashore flowers and corn grew. The Celts had close contacts with the Greeks and their own mythology reflects a similar story. Venus came from the sea, but was primarily an Earth goddess. She was known as 'Tailltiu' to the Irish Celts and was buried beneath the great earth mound at Tailtenn in Ireland. Tailltiu was a very primitive Earth goddess, who later evolved into their Triple Goddess of Maiden–Mother–Hag.

The Empress is the Mother aspect of the Goddess and

associated with their summer festival of Beltane, celebrated on the first of May. It was the most important aspect of fertility, and her purple dress signifies her divine status. She was called 'Queen of the May' or 'Queen Maeve of the Sidhe'. The Sidhe were the Faery people in Celtic legends who lived underground in secret caverns. They were known to carry off children in order to teach them the skills and art of the Sidhe. The planet Venus (or Celtic 'Gwena') is also associated with the arts and all skilled craftwork.

Her necklace has been further enlarged to show the unique Celtic sense of beauty and craft in a traditional manner. Jewellery was perhaps their finest example of a perfected art form. The triple design incorporated with carnelian stones was a protective talisman against witchcraft and ill-health. The nine pearls were sacred to

Gwena and associated with the nine virgins who attended her.

The twelve silver stars in the background are symbolic of the twelve constellations of the Zodiac, and represents her universal role as a great civilizing force on all nations. The two pillars of intertwining corn are associated with the fertility of earth, and symbolic of the role of the Empress as 'Patroness of the Arts' in refining the nature of mankind. But the craft of homemaking and motherhood remains the most creative skill of all. All the skills, however, hold the standards of civilization which could not evolve or advance without them.

This is a card which signifies initiative and success. There is an association with pleasure and the pursuit of the arts which can appear excessive or sensual. But in its highest form, art is a spiritual experience that enriches the soul. The Empress has an unknown quality which does rely on the spiritual nature of the querent. It promises much, but the sensual nature of the individual has to overcome the undercurrent of earthly passion.

Dignified It reveals a fine appreciation of the arts and an understanding of the practical skills or labour involved. When this card is drawn the querent may also be involved with the construction of something pertaining to the arts, but it can be associated with successful enterprises of any kind. Motherhood may be the most important role at present, but it can also represent the fruitful labour of both men and women.

Ill-dignified It can mean doubt of own worth, also idleness and ignorance. The querent may be experiencing some difficulties in expressing the finer qualities or skills necessary to adjust to life. But it is not an evil or difficult card generally speaking. The neighbouring cards would have to be very disruptive or evil in their intent to displace this card.

The Empress combines the highest spiritual quest with the lowest or more earthly qualities and pursuits of mankind.

The Emperor

The Emperor sits on a throne resplendent in the vestments of power and authority. He is holding in one hand a sceptre — a ceremonial staff which still commands like a wand the invisible forces of the spiritual realm. In his other hand, the orb now proclaims his allegiance to the Christian God. Here is Arthur Pendragon, Cornish king of the Dumnonii — a Celtic people who lived in Cornwall and Devon during the so-called 'Dark Ages' of 400-1066 AD. A legendary ruler, perhaps, but in the hearts and

minds of the Celtic people he undoubtedly existed, and was later romanticized in both Norman and Saxon chronicles.

The circular emblem immediately behind him is a significant reminder of the Round Table and the order of valiant knights who helped to maintain his rule of law and justice. The curious face revealed between the jaws of two serpents above him has a strange impassive expression which reflects the Celtic sense of mystery. The quest of the Holy Grail was the most intriguing mystery of all the Arthurian legends. According to this legend Joseph of Arimathea had brought the secret of the Holy Grail to Cornwall and given it to Bran the Blessed. Another mythical figure perhaps, but the singing head of Bran was said to have been preserved, and later venerated, by pilgrims eager to witness its strange powers of healing. Bran has also been linked with Janus, an ancient Celtic god of the Underworld, whose cult was associated with the regeneration of the soul — or a re-birth through mysterious rites.

Is it the mystical Head of Bran? It invites a question mark — but it is perhaps a good example of the depth and breadth of the spiritual consciousness of the Celtic people.

The two rams' heads on either side of the throne are associated with the astrological sign of Aries and the Vernal Equinox — 21st March. This was a festival associated with male gods in the pre-Christian Celtic calendar; a time when the King of the Celts harnessed the masculine energy of fire, the solar energy of creative power. In a sacred ritual, he symbolically regenerated the strength of his people and established the order of the seasons. A stabilizing force, like Arthur, who originated some of the early codes of conduct of a Christian knight.

The Emperor card deals with order and stability, reason and the realization of responsibility, albeit in personal or administrative terms. It relates to the father of the querent in a personal sense, but also to an authoritative power which can be the governing forces in society generally. It provides aid, a strengthening of convictions or attitudes. It can also mean a benefactor who will help the querent.

Dignified It reveals a need to show compassion even in victory. The querent's course of action is deemed correct. A strength of character has been established, and the way ahead is more encouraging now the querent has learned to obey the rules so to speak. This is a particularly good card to draw if the querent has been experiencing a lack of self-confidence: it reveals a definite ambition or skill which will surface and harness the creative energy within.

Ill-dignified There still exists an immaturity within the character of the querent. Too much energy is wasted on argument and strife. The impulsive nature is not checked; hasty and angry words are being exchanged which are exhausting the mind and body. Accidents occur, again through too much haste, and by not seeing things objectively. Obstacles suddenly appear.

The Emperor card is the corresponding card to The Empress. It is not, however, a spiritual guide, but more concerned with establishing a solid base of action in the material world.

The Hierophant

The Hierophant sits on a different throne to the Emperor — the spiritual throne of Holy Office. The Emperor had power over the temporal world, but the Hierophant is responsible for the soul. The triple-cross sceptre held in one hand is a traditional Christian symbol connecting the seven rounded points of the cross to the seven deadly sins. The Hierophant is associated with the Pope or Head

of Church in Christianity, but it is not exclusively a Christian Dignity. The Hierophant is the spiritual leader over all orthodox religions which have been established around the world.

The Celtic Church had long established traditions starting from the fifth century AD and during the Dark Ages continued to send missionaries across the continent of Europe, even back to Rome. The Celtic people had identified the coming of Christ with a Druid prophecy, which was a fulfilment of their ancient belief in Druidism. The figure of the Hierophant raising the other hand is a traditional Druid blessing of two pointed fingers held by the crossed thumb, adopted by Christian priests. The Celts themselves were a very adaptable people, but they recognized the power of Christ and were early converts whilst still retaining their own highly-evolved spirituality.

The crimson robe has holy status, and the chain of office has the sign of the crucifix fashioned in a traditional Celtic design. The two circles conjoined with the cross represent the power of Christ over both the temporal and spiritual world. The two lambs' heads above the Hierophant are a Christian symbol of Christ, the Lamb of God. This is perhaps a more significant symbol than is immediately obvious. There is associated with the Hierophant a need for self-sacrifice.

The two figures with hands clasped in prayer are kneeling at the feet of the Hierophant, a sign of servitude and devotion which represents the whole significance of the Hierophant. The Hierophant is a teacher, and the figures represent the instruction of the card — that of listening.

This card deals with learning and listening, a time for pause in the querent's life. The Hierophant may represent a person or personage in the life of the querent who becomes a source of inspiration. It is also associated with marriage — the sanctity of marriage, which is the bonding of two spirits, rather than the legal status. The astrological sign associated with this card is Taurus and the corresponding sign in the Druid Zodiac of sacred trees is The Willow. It was a tree associated with enchantment and the gift of mystical vision. In more general terms it reinforces the inspiration of personal loyalty to others and to God. If the querent is an atheist or an agnostic, it symbolizes the need to question the motives or principles of the querent.

Dignified If related to the querent it shows a firm set of values and a trustworthy character. If the querent is married and is facing some problems, this card reinforces the vows of marriage and reminds the querent of their obligations. It shows the strength of that marriage, which should not be underestimated.

Ill-dignified A resentful attitude exists concerning a partner or a current situation in the life of the querent. Greed, self-indulgence and not listening to reason may be the root cause of the matter. If drawn as an influencing force or a person connected with the querent, it means the querent should show tolerance and mercy — which may be difficult in the circumstances.

The Hierophant, like the High Priestess, is a source of inspiration. The Hierophant is, however, concerned with establishing a belief — unlike the more fluid and mystical force of the High Priestess.

The Lovers

The two lovers are encapsulated forever in their own time warp. Time for lovers has a different meaning and dimension: time will stand still, or so they say. The lovers' illusion of time is perhaps not an illusion at all, but a deeper insight into the dual energies which control the nature of all things. The naked couple are celebrating their union as the man offers the woman a draught of wine from a drinking horn. The romance of Tristan and Iseult is immediately visualized, and the Celtic heart exposed.

The story of Tristan and Iseult began with a magic love-potion concealed in a flagon of wine. Tristan, a Celtic knight and nephew of King Mark of Cornwall, had been sent to fetch the fair Iseult, daughter of the King of Ireland, as a bride for King Mark. Their ship became becalmed and a serving maid accidentally opened the wine which had been specially brewed to ensure a love-match between Iseult and her future husband. The Celtic tribes of Cornwall and Ireland had been engaged in bitter conflict and the marriage was seen as an important truce and hope of a lasting alliance. The love-potion had been obtained by Iseult's mother from a Druidess of Faery blood.

But the plans of mortals are often upstaged in mythology by the Gods, and the fated love-potion became a fatal dose of love. Tristan and Iseult were eventually parted through a series of tragic misunderstandings, and both died alone — for the love of the other.

Love stories often have tragic endings, but the story of Tristan and Iseult was of their enduring love for each other, despite the anger it had evoked in others — and for a time between themselves.

The mercurial Cupid firing the arrows is the divine intervention which inspires love and passion in equal measure, for one cannot be stronger than the other or the delicate alchemical balance turns to lust and hate.

This is represented astrologically by the sign of Gemini — associated with the Oak Tree in the Celtic division of the Zodiac. Trees were sacred to the Druids, and the oak was regarded as the most sacred of all, not only for its strength and beauty, but also because the sacred mistletoe grew in its boughs. Mistletoe was a symbol of life not growing directly from the earth, and the berries were silver pearls — the essence of life not to be touched by man. The Druids cut the mistletoe with great reverence and used the berries for healing barrenness in women and animals.

The tree shown in the card is rooted between the lovers, but its fruit-bearing branches are spread above them as a reminder not to pick such fruits without considering the consequence. The brilliance of the Sun is a symbol of Creation — the key significance of the card.

Dignified It brings together the best aspects of a partnership in both men and women. It can also inspire love in both sexes, but not homosexual love, because the lovers are symbolic of the dual or polarity of energies. It can inspire a brotherly or sisterly love which transcends the sexual aspect. If the querent is single and attracted to a new partner, this card promises a deeper understanding of that relationship. If already married it shows that any problems within the marriage will be resolved.

Ill-dignified It shows a frustration in a personal relationship. There exists a division which creates uncertainty for both parties. It has not yet deteriorated entirely, however, and matters can be resolved — providing there is still the will to do so.

The Lovers is primarily a card of great rapport and understanding. Lovers' tiffs etc. may occur but can be a case of mistiming.

The Chariot

The Chariot is a card of action, but the Charioteer has perfect control of all the elements and energies of the

The Chariot.

universe. The mightiest hero and charioteer of the Celtic race, Cuchulain, was born with a Druid's prophecy. The prophecy contained the message of the card, and went thus: 'His praise will be in the mouths of all men; charioteers and warriors, kings and sages will recount his deeds; he will win the love of many. This child will avenge all your wrongs; he will give combat at your fords, he will decide your quarrels.'[1]

Cuchulain was a great warrior, but he always showed mercy and great gallantry in a Celtic manner. He had defeated a fierce warrior princess called Aifa, and they became lovers for a brief interlude. As a parting gift she

[1] T. W. Rolleston, *Myths and Legends of the Celtic Race* (London: George G. Harrap 1987).

had given him the legendary chariot and horses. No other chariot had been better crafted, and the horses had no equal in speed or courage. The silver grey horse was called the Grey of Macha and the powerful black steed was called Black Sainglend. They are shown in the card in the true colour of spirit — amethyst and silver blue.

The Charioteer stands impassive, holding the wand of power and a bolt of lightning to control the galloping horses. His green tunic, with a blue and gold robe, are symbolic colours of Mercy and Strength.

Cuchulain was strong and merciful, but he had killed his only son in battle — a cruel irony for such a valiant warrior, who did not know at the time the true identity of his young opponent. Only as the youth lay dying, did he reveal his name of Connla, and his mother was no other than the proud warrior Princess Aifa. She had concealed the name of his father to protect him from her people, who still hated the name Cuchulain. Connla was the name Cuchulain had asked the Princess to call their child should it be a boy.

This tragic twist of fate is another significant factor of the card. The traditional astrological sign associated with the card is Cancer. In the Druid Zodiac, Cancer is represented by the Holly Tree, a symbol of spiritual development, but the Moon rules Cancer and holds the key to past deeds and the inherited traits of character.

This card deals with situations which tend to recur. A residue of the past confronts the querent in an effort to shake off the shadows which still exist. Cuchulain had met 'his past' without knowing it — until too late. Swift action is often necessary when this card is drawn, but the lesson of Cuchulain is a reminder to 'know thine enemy' and to recognize past errors of judgement and not make the same mistakes again. For, in order to proceed like the Charioteer, the querent must be in full control of the situation.

Dignified It shows victory of a kind, but not without some thorough soul-searching. Health and vitality will also improve once the querent identifies the root cause of the problem. Family matters are important issues and progress can be made to settle any disputes or long-standing divisions. Compromise is the key to regaining the initiative.

Ill-dignified Violent recriminations will follow any action of the querent. The querent may become involved in litigation proceedings and lose the case. Quarrels and disputes occur over trivial matters and no headway is made on more important matters. There is also a tendency to dwell on past issues with negative results.

The Chariot is a forceful card, designed to provoke action in order to contain it. This might sound contradictory, but stagnant energies create their own chaos when swift action is required to stop the rot.

Strength

The young woman holds the jaws of the beast to demonstrate her power over the uncontrolled forces of nature. The wild beast shown is the Celtic equivalent to the Lion, a beast traditionally associated with the card of Strength. This is not physical strength, but a determination to work to good purpose. Her pale grey-blue robe is the esoteric or spiritual colour of Strength. To interpret the significance of this gesture, the Celtic legend of Queen Macha is a relevant comparison.

As a young girl, Macha had power and strength equal to any man. She fought and slew her brother Dithorba to rule Ireland in her own right. Her slender stature and fragile beauty belied her formidable strength of character. She was known as 'Queen Macha of the Red or Golden Hair'.

On the first of August, a great festival was celebrated in her honour in Emain, where she had founded a palace. There is a fertility aspect of the Triple Goddess associated with this date, which indicates the sexual force or drive — contained within the image of a young girl subduing the forces of nature or man — to conceive.

There are many legends concerning Queen Macha. Her beauty became a sinister aspect of her strength when she appeared in battle. Her bright, flashing eyes were as deadly as a serpent's and made men freeze with horror. She is linked in Celtic mythology to the intermingling of the people of Danaan ancestry with the human race.

The Danaan people were the Faery people, and have been described as radiantly beautiful, but they wielded their power from sorcery and enchantment. They did not die naturally, but could be slain by each other and by some

mortals. Their powers of strength were supernatural, which is again symbolic of the card. It is a time when extraordinary force is required to overcome a weakening aspect of character or a force that pervades the querent.

The vivid characters in Celtic mythology have a unique blend of mortal and immortal qualities. It is a record of their own evolving nature, which the Celtic Wheel behind the young Queen symbolizes. It holds the intricate energies of Earth, and requires a strength of purpose to recognize and to master. The Celts expressed their flamboyant nature in their art with great sensitivity and style.

The card Strength has also been called Justice, and this perhaps conveys a truer image when using the Tarot for divination. For Strength is the Sword Arm of Justice, if it is to be used wisely and mercifully. It also reveals a time when consolidating action is required, not just the pretence of action.

Dignified It shows an honourable cause or objective. The querent will be successful, providing he or she does not lack the courage to face up to adversities. The power of leadership is shown, which enables the querent to take charge of a situation. Sexual motivation is another aspect which could be relevant. It is a very positive card overall and will detract from some of the difficult forces of the surrounding cards.

Ill-dignified The abuse of power is self-evident. Disgrace occurs, both personally and in the public sector. Seeds of discord are sown — weakness and cowardice prevail.

The card of Strength illustrates an important principle: people who retreat from a difficult situation will also inevitably lose their strength of purpose and will-power — so the life force will be weakened.

The Hermit

Walking barefoot, a sign of deep humility, The Fool re-enters the scene having completed part of his journey. The Hermit's figure of an old man, wearing the red robe, is symbolic of having completed a cycle of spiritual evolution in the esoteric sense. He is Merlin in Celtic mythology, an evolved soul who held the light of conscience for his race. He taught King Arthur Pendragon of Cornwall the craft of true kingship — to serve as well as to rule the people. The Hermit is a solitary figure in the spiritual sense, but it can be the means of perfecting the self-discipline so necessary to evolve at all.

Merlin holds a lamp to light the way for others and its light is reflected from the solar disc, the light of Creation. The staff he carries is the Staff of Faith, a symbol of

allegiance to God. The Hermit is a Holy man, hence the association with religion, but the card can also signify an adherence to understanding the fundamental principles by which to live a good and honest life. The Hermit's lamp is symbolic of finding a path through life without the darkness and despair of loneliness which pervades the souls of all mankind.

The Celts lived during a period of history when man was still experiencing the darkness of ignorance and super-stition. Their religion is not easily defined, but followed a series of assimilating various cultures, starting with the Megalithic peoples, who built the great stone monuments and occupied Western Europe from Scandinavia to the Straits of Gibraltar, to the ancient Greeks, whose own origins are equally obscure. Druidism certainly evolved in Britain, and eventually became a centre of learning for all Druids.

The astrological sign of Virgo is associated with this card — the Celtic sign of The Vine. It symbolizes a critical self-awareness, a need to discover and eliminate imper-fections of character. The driving force is servitude and abstinence — a cleansing programme designed to purify the soul. The sign of Virgo is also linked to vegetarian beliefs, a practice or way of life followed by the Druids.

This card certainly deals with prudence and discrimi-nation. The querent has reached an important period in his or her life. The path ahead may indeed be a lonely one if he or she decides to follow the spirit of the card. In more practical terms, querents may decide to serve others in the community with a renewed faith. The essence of the card is difficult to define for the individual. Like religion, it can evoke a tremendous faith or leave the querent even more determined to go his or her own way.

Dignified It shows an acceptance of self-worth. A point of self-realization has been reached. Divine inspiration is forthcoming, which strengthens resolve. Wisdom of the soul becomes an individual asset, and provides a vital clue to a greater wisdom and vision. The querent may have already experienced the 'loneliness' of The Hermit and be ready to teach others.

Ill-dignified The cautious side of nature becomes miserly and austere. The querent is denying an important principle and lacks true faith. The querent is closing his or her heart and mind for the wrong reasons. True abstinence is a virtue, but it can become the means of denying love to self, family and friends.

The Hermit symbolizes a part of the soul which is the most difficult to come to terms with. It represents the imperfections which need to be brought out into the open and dispersed once and for all.

Wheel of Fortune

The Morrigan, the Celtic Fate-Goddess, holds the Wheel of Fortune card in her hand. This most awesome, but most prophetic aspect of the Lunar Goddess, held the supernatural powers which decided man's fate. The Morrigan could change into many frightful shapes and hovered over battlefields as a crow or raven. She delighted in setting men at war, and would often join in the battle, changing into snarling beasts or monstrous creatures. She appears to embody all the perverse and horrible aspects of nature and man, the darker element of the invisible phase of the Moon.

The three symbols of the Moon above the Celtic Wheel of Life show the Dark Moon, the New Moon and the Full Moon. The Dark Moon or the infernal Moon is the Lunar Goddess in her triple aspect of the Hag or the Morrigan. Fatality has always been associated with the Moon on the decrease, and the Celtic Druids were keen observers of the astronomical influences. The Morrigan was a fearful spectre to behold, but she holds the card or key that will open the doors of knowledge or those regions of hell that contain the answers or solutions to the Wheel of Life.

The Wheel of Fortune is a title of the Tarot card which indicates the flux of human endeavours within the Wheel of Life. The Wheel is an ancient symbol of life itself and the four elements shown within the wheel are symbols of the four Evangelists: Matthew, Mark, Luke and John. Similar symbols are shown in the famous manuscript, *The Book of Kells,* a record of illustrations and writings produced in about the eighth century by the monasteries in the British Isles. The origins are not certain because of the diverse development of the Christian Church in Celtic Britain.

Apart from proclaiming the classical skills of the Celtic monk or priest, it shows the highly evolved spiritual dimension of the Celtic mind. The four Evangelists represent the four stages or cycles of man which correspond with Christ's life. The Man is Matthew, whose gospel dealt with the arrest of Christ. The sign of the Lion is Mark, and represents the Crucifixion. The Calf is Luke, a symbol of Temptation. The Eagle is John, a sign of the Resurrection. Interpreted through the Wheel of Life, Man decides his course of action, pays the penalty or accepts his fate, has to acknowledge his weaker aspects, and finally emerges like the eagle or the phoenix rising from the ashes. The Wheel does hold the power of life and death, but not in the physical sense.

The planet Jupiter (known as Jovyn to the Celts) is the element of luck attached to this card. For all the ups and downs in life, this card does signify a new beginning or a new chance to do something rather special — a chance to evolve and not to be drawn into the downward spiral of the Morrigan.

Dignified: It shows good fortune and the destiny of the querent looks very promising. Success or accomplishment is the upward turn of the Wheel. The querent may suddenly be given the opportunity to excel, but it is the result of his or her own deeds, past and present. The time is ripe for making changes in the life of the querent, an important factor which needs to be fully understood.

Ill-dignified There is an increase in the weaker aspects of character. The downward spiral creates uncertainty and blind optimism. The neighbouring cards point to the extent of this fall, but the Wheel of Fortune creates opportunities sometimes at the expense of others. Hence the negative aspect of this card does depend on the neighbouring cards, which show the preceding influence or situation.

The Wheel of Fortune is an optimistic card and has a higher significance than dealing with the good or bad luck of the querent. It shows a deeper understanding of the exact direction in which the querent is heading.

Justice

The Celtic queen holding the Scales of Justice and the Sword of Lugh is Queen Dana, mother of the gods who invaded Ireland around the late Bronze Age. They were called the 'Tuatha De Danann' which means *'the folk of the god whose mother is Dana'*. This branch of early Celts had brought with them four great treasures: The Lia Fail, or Stone of Destiny; the Sword of Lugh; the Spear of Finias; and the Magic Cauldron of Dagda. The card of Justice is

a symbol of the sword and the scales, which represent a balance of mercy and retribution. The sword can be a swift retribution if the scales are tipped against the querent.

But the double edge of the sword has a dual purpose: it can disperse the negative dross which has accumulated and liberate the mind, or reinforce the power of reason which already exists. The scales weigh up the good and bad points of character or the deeds of the querent. The spiritual significance is an important factor to consider, for the Major Arcana cards of the Tarot represent the symbolic pictures of the soul.

The Celtic queen is dressed in the finery of her rank and position. The gold torque necklace is a symbol of obedience to a higher power who administers justice over all mankind. Her red robe is a symbolic colour of strength or positive thought. Her cloak of bright orange reinforces the energies of colour, the vibrant forces surrounding her.

The two jackals at her feet hold in their jaws both ends of the cord of life, which forms a labyrinth of possibilities. Like the ancient Greeks, the Celts were intrigued with the meaning of life and the endless possibilities or voyages of discovery it provoked. The association with the labyrinth picks up the quest of man: the search for immortality. The astrological sign of Libra is associated with the card of Justice. The Druids called this sign The Ivy and it represented the growth of the Evergreen or the immortality of the soul.

This card introduces the idea of reincarnation. The action of the querent requires adjustment, not only in the present life, but on the evolutionary Wheel of Life. Justice has been called 'Adjustment', an esoteric title which best describes the action required of the querent. It is also associated with legal proceedings in the courts, trials involving the laws of the land in which the querent resides. Libra is a sign of partnerships, and such trials often involve disputes in marriages or business partnerships.

Dignified It shows a fair judgement for the querent. Whatever that judgement may be, e.g. a pending court case or a legal settlement, the querent will be favourably dealt with. On a higher spiritual level, a sign of approval will be felt, which releases the querent from an imbalance of the soul. The neighbouring cards will determine the form of justice or the level of adjustment required.

Ill-dignified Complications will occur which impede justice. Bigotry and bias judgements reflect the querent's own mismanagement of his or her affairs. Severe penalties or fines are imposed.

The card of Justice is an indictment of all the aspects of the querent's life. It demonstrates the conscious need to redress the balance or the equilibrium state of mind, which the Air element of Libra controls.

The Hanged Man

The Hanged Man is a strange and curious figure, hanging suspended upside down by one ankle. His silver-blue tunic and harlequin trousers are symbolic of The Fool, but he is now controlled by the element of Water. He is looking at the world from a completely new perspective. This significant reversal creates an air of mystery and curiosity. The intention of the Hanged Man is to show that there is another way of looking at life or the situation confronting the querent.

In Celtic mythology this type of suspended animation was associated with Arianrhod, a Lunar Goddess. The British Celts were an island race who had observed how the Moon controlled the tidal flow of the sea. Water was the element of life; it meant trade and contact with the outside world. But their perceptive nature also recognized the undercurrents or the magical energies of the Moon.

The mystical quality of moonlight cast a spell which enveloped their senses.

The Druids were adepts at shape-changing, an extraordinary phenomenon not readily believed today. It was merely a demonstration of the power that lies dormant, coiled like a sea-serpent, in all men and women. The symbol of the Sea-serpent is the structure on which the Hanged Man is attached. The association with water is a spiritual one, for the card is touching on matters which have a mysterious or unknown origin.

Arianrhod was also known to the ancient Greeks as the Spider Goddess — Ariadne or Arachne. The Spider Goddess was an ancient cult figure and deals with the psychic nature of man. The Hanged Man dangling by a thread resembles the spider's vision of the world. Mental telepathy and levitation is the imagery of the card — a need to explore the realms of consciousness as yet untapped. Ancient civilizations had perhaps a keener awareness or vision of the subterranean levels of consciousness.

The golden disc around the Hanged Man's head is a solar symbol of the Sacrificed God. The Celts had identified Jesus with their Druidic belief of a sacrificial Sun-god. The golden disc or halo was transferred to their early Christian saints, who usually suffered the fate of martyrs.

This card represents making a sacrifice of some kind in order to see things more clearly. The position of the querent is hanging on a thread quite literally — not so precarious as The Fool, but certainly a time to reverse matters which are getting out of control. A card to reflect upon, no easy solutions or answers are found in the Hanged Man. The element of water can be a reflective mirror or an uncontrolled and distorted torrent, a force which shatters all illusions.

Dignified It shows a newly-aligned wisdom. The querent rediscovers his or her own divinity. The intuitive nature and senses are awakened — life has more meaning and colour. The querent has accepted a difficult situation and made the necessary sacrifices — an unselfish act. A spiritual revelation transforms the consciousness, a prophetic state of mind exists.

Ill-dignified Suffering is apparent. Great distress generally is felt by the querent. Loss of friends, loss of faith, a cycle of losing what matters most. Sacrifices made are not voluntary, but enforced by others. Life becomes suspended — a state of limbo exists where the querent is powerless to make a move.

The Hanged Man is a radical force which encourages an alternative choice or perspective — a reminder of the psychic nature of things which defy reason.

Death

The skeletal spectre of Death arrives by boat, wrapped in the mysterious cloak of Manannan. The dead are then conveyed back to the Land of Youth by a sea-god, who changes his appearance with his magic cloak to create the grim aspect of Death. But the journey about to begin is the transmigration of the soul — according to Celtic belief. Drawings of solar ships have been discovered on standing stones in Brittany and Ireland which are identical to early Egyptian hieroglyphics denoting the Cult of the Dead — a belief in the immortality of the soul.

Julius Caesar had dismissed the Celts as a semi-barbarous people, but he had been impressed by their Druids' knowledge of medicine and scholarly learning. He had been particularly fascinated to discover the Druids'

view of death was similar to Pythagoras' and wrote: 'The principle point of their [the Druids'] teaching is that the soul does not perish, and after death — it passes from one body into another.'

These few lines pick up the idea of the Death card — a transition of life rather than physical death. Death is a disturbing card however; it indicates having to suffer some kind of loss, which can be a devastating experience. The astrological sign of Scorpio, a Water sign, is attributed to Death, and the Druids identified it as the sign of The Reed. A symbol of being submerged in water and yet retaining the ability to breathe is another significant comparison.

One of the two figures waiting on the shore is King Arthur, and the lady holding the lamp represents the new dawn of Christianity. To the Celts, King Arthur represented an important time of transition in their own evolutionary journey. King Arthur was the first great Christian King of the Celtic people, and his meeting with Death is symbolic of a new Golden Age about to begin.

Ancient Britain was considered by the Gauls and continental tribes to be a sacred burial place of 'the Gods', and a place where gods still roamed on earth. A glimpse of the ghostly white cliffs, and the sudden descent of mist which hovered over the dividing water, was enough to keep intruding races away for several centuries. The Breton fishermen today still talk about the legend of ferrying their dead over to shores of 'Alba Longa' — the name of ancient Britain.

The mysterious figure-head of the boat is the Celtic god Janus, the God of the Underworld, whose role was as both a guardian and initiator of Death. The mermaid figure swimming alongside the boat is reminiscent of the Lady of the Lake, as she raises her arm to greet Arthur. Her presence perhaps defines something of the mystical element of Death.

Dignified It indicates a transformation of a situation that can herald new beginnings. Past events have finally been brought under control and the querent can make the changes necessary to live or to evolve rather than remain cocooned in the past.

Ill-dignified The querent is lacking real purpose and seeks an easy way out of a current situation. Not facing up to a situation will create a destructive cycle for self and others. Loss of life or property cannot be ruled out if the neighbouring cards are negative.

The Death card is an important point of self-realization; it raises the question of whether to hang on to something not worth having. The symbol of the rising Sun in the card is a reminder that something is both finished and about to begin all over again.

Temperance

The Angel of Temperance appears as a mediator and a great healing force. A radiant vision of light and love, she pours the elixir of life from one vase to another to balance an unequal load. The Celts had many healing wells and sacred springs. Water was the lifeforce of Creation, the sacred blood of their Earth Goddess. The healing properties of such wells and springs have effected some remarkable cures over the centuries.

There are in Cornwall alone nearly 200 wells and springs which lie mostly forgotten. One particular spring is the Holy Well of St Keyne, an early Celtic saint renowned for her strength of purity and radiant beauty. She toured the whole of Britain performing many miracles of healing and changing serpents into stone. When she became too old to travel, she settled in Cornwall and lived in the beautiful valley that bears her name. Over the spring she planted the four most sacred trees of the Druids — oak, ash, elm and a willow — endowing the waters with their peculiar virtues. As she lay dying, she blessed the spring by praying for peace on earth above all things.

The early Celtic saints still retained a mystical aura and St Keyne had demonstrated the powers and knowledge of a Druidess. Her royal bloodline confirms this point — her father, King Brychan, was of Welsh Druidic lineage. The success of Christianity had the backing of such Druids and Druidesses. The sacred wells of their Goddess became Holy Wells, which signified their transference of power, rather than a conversion of Christianity.

The astrological sign of Sagittarius is traditionally associated with the Temperance card. The mythical ruler of this sign in Greek mythology was Cheiron, the fabled half-man, half-horse, from the race of Centaurs. Cheiron

was also a tutor to the children of the Gods and great heroes. He taught them many wondrous things, but his greatest gift was the knowledge of healing. The Druids also attributed to this sign two trees renowned for their healing properties — Elder and Myrtle. Both are venerated in folklore herbalism and still used today by practising herbalists.

The rising Sun, symbolic of life regenerating, describes the card very well. The powerful rays send forth beacons of light which purify and cleanse the whole psyche. The angelic figure symbolically places one foot into the healing waters to signify the healer being healed. This relates to an ancient legend of the Lamed Fisher King who, in Celtic mythology, like Cheiron could not heal his own wound. When this card is drawn it suggests the querent has to overcome a personal weakness in order to help others. Tempering is part of the action of temperance, and it suggests a need to correct an ill-temper. There is a health factor also connected with this card which indicates excesses of food and drink.

Dignified It shows honesty, propriety and the ability to help others. The querent may be drawn to joining groups concerned with the welfare of the less fortunate, e.g. the Samaritans. It also indicates a period in the querent's life where careful management is very necessary for their own health. Convalescence after an illness is progressing well.

Ill-dignified A meanness of spirit prevails, also regarding material matters. Alternatively, the querent cannot see the need to cut wasteful expenditure which will eventually create debt and bankruptcy. Moderation is required in all spheres of life to counterbalance the self-indulgent nature of the querent.

The Temperance card is a warning to curb excesses in life, but it also signifies a healing process — peace on earth to all mankind.

The Devil

The Celtic Wheel of Life is momentarily held in check by the reversed pentacle, a sign of evil or the Devil. The face of the Devil peers out from the pentacle with a sardonic smile of greeting. He does not look particularly menacing, but he is obviously enjoying the spectacle of the two figures on their knees in front of him. They have been caught in a state of undress, which suggests an illicit love-affair or a lustful act. To add to their indignity, a demon dances gleefully around them as he plays the pipes of Pan. The demon holds aloft the chains that bind them together, as he manipulates the figures like a puppeteer.

But take a closer look at the chains: the couple could break free, if they were not blinded by their shameful passion. The Devil was invented by the Christian Church

to symbolize temptation and the weakness of the flesh.
The Celtic people were less inhibited, and accepted the
fact that demons were an integral part of life. They called
one great demon Cenchos — the Footless One. This huge
serpent-like figure, who had neither feet nor hands,
brought pestilence and darkened the sky with its foul
breath. A loathsome creature, but it was more concerned
with destroying man physically, than the more subtle
overtures of the Christian Devil.

But as the Celts became Christianized, their understanding of the Devil also changed. They began to use
their ancient Druidic powers to fight the Devil at every
opportunity. Many early Celtic saints were descendants of
the Druids, and their stunning feats of magic helped to
convert the people. The power of the Devil appeared to
grow however, and eventually he was considered by the
dualists or heretics to be the brother of Jesus — no longer
the dark, fallen angel Lucifer described in the early
gospels, but the twin brother or dual God, who ruled the
material world of the flesh. The Christian zeal for
promoting Jesus had perhaps unwittingly promoted or
elevated the Devil.

The white hares depicted in the sidelines are bound
more tightly, and escape is less certain. They represent the
innocent victims who often suffer in silence, but their
fearful expression shows the pain being inflicted. The
Devil shown in this card has an aura of wicked intent, but
it is not such a malefic force if studied carefully. It is a
reflection of our own evil intent — nothing more. It is easy
to blame the Devil in the same way as the early Christians
did. But this card deals with the negative aspects of
character which need to be recognized and dealt with.

The astrological sign of Capricorn is associated with
this card and corresponds with the Birch Tree in the Druid
Zodiac. In days since past, birching was another name for
whipping or punishing an offender, an apt comparison
when dealing with the Devil.

Dignified Not a good card to draw at any time. At best it shows the querent is aware of a negative situation and is endeavouring to shake off the chains which bind him or her. It may be that an illicit love-affair has been exposed and the querent is seeking to rectify the matter. Temptation is being resisted, but a difficult situation exists.

Ill-dignified Violence or death may occur. Death is not the evil outcome, but the result of a force which can no longer be contained. A weakness or a negative attitude exists which blinds the querent to his or her own faults and also to the actions of others.

The Devil has a sinister aspect, but it is a card which exposes the negative or misplaced energies and loyalties of the querent.

The Tower

The Tower is a powerfully evocative card; it breathes disaster and the wrath of God. It is traditionally linked to the Tower of Babel mentioned in the Bible and in other ancient records. Berosus, a Babylonian priest and historian, wrote a book on man's early origins which is very similar to the Book of Genesis. In his version of the Tower of Babel it had been built by Nimrod for Solomon, and contained all the knowledge of the world. It was a fabulous library, and its destruction was a warning from God not to evolve from knowledge alone. Knowledge becomes impotent unless interpreted with wisdom and humility. The Tower, in this sense, represents the construction of false ideals and values.

The round towers of Ireland are associated with the Culdees, an early Christian priesthood who wore the white robes of the Druids, but practised a strange mixture of Paganism and Christianity. They were active mostly in Ireland, Scotland and Wales, the strongholds of Celtic culture and thinking. Although they were shunned by the orthodox Church of Rome and many other British bishops, they managed to survive from the ninth century to the sixteenth century AD. The Christian monks and priests who opposed them believed the tower constructions of the Culdees represented the Tower of Babel — a symbol of the Church of the old religion — paganism. Along with the ill-fated Templar Knights, the Culdees were accused of worshipping the powers of darkness and of making all manner of human sacrifices, as were their Druidic forefathers.

The Culdees were perhaps holding on to the remnants of Druidism which had not yet evolved, and remained a lower cultus of spiritual development. The Celtic Church also disputed many points of theology and the practice of Christianity with the Roman Church. It believed priests could marry, did not object to the participation of women during mass and celebrated Easter at a different date. But they finally agreed to merge and form a united front. The Reformation Act centuries later gave birth to the Protestant Church, a significant reminder that compromise is not always the best answer. Two diverse ways of thinking are channels of energy which need to run their own course. The Tower deals with matters that have no solid or safe foundations and is directly linked to unstable energies.

The planet associated with this card is Mars, known as Merth to the Celts, and in all ancient mythology as the God of War. The action of Mars when linked to the Tower is swift and sudden. It shatters illusions and false hopes — an extreme action, but a regenerating force in the long term.

The two people falling from the tower are still desperately trying to hang on to something they believe in — like the Culdees. The false crown of hope at the top of the tower is, however, being struck down by the overwhelming force from above. It shows it is time to let go of worthless ideals and values.

Dignified Always a sign of a pending disaster. The neighbouring cards may mitigate the scale of the disaster, but it would be prudent to listen to good advice at this time. Minor disasters may be linked to electrical goods suddenly breaking down due to bad maintenance. The querent may also expect some violent opposition from others at this time.

Ill-dignified A sudden unexpected calamity will occur. It could be redundancy at work, financial ruin or a personal setback regarding ambitions; or disputes at work and in the domestic life of the querent which suddenly escalate and cause a division.

The Tower is a purging force, but not necessarily a des-

tructive force. The querent must move forward and recon-
struct his or her life.

The Star

The Star is a card of hope and a symbol of the universal
beauty of nature. The circular wheel is a cosmic mirror
reflecting the pentacle, a symbol of Earth in perfect
harmony, with the seven stars representing the universe.
The Dove of Peace is flying upwards towards the highest
point of the pentacle to signify the soaring spirit of man.

  The pentacle touching the circle of the universe is a five-
pointed star and associated with the five magic symbols
of light and hope in Celtic mythology. They were recorded
thus: 'The living fiery spear of Lugh, the magic ship of

Manannan, the singing sword of Conery Mor, Cuchulain's sword which spoke, and the Lia Fail, Stone of Destiny'. Each one represented a divine aspect of God through which man could rule on earth.

The figure of the naked lady clothed in the purple robe is carefully pouring the healing waters of Aquarius. The water from the two vases is poured in equal measure on earth, and back into its own element of Water, a symbol of the source of life. Aquarius is traditionally associated with the Star and signifies a universal consciousness and the uniqueness of man. In astrology, the Aquarian vision is a progressive one, a reforming spirit with humanitarian principles, a healing force in its highest form.

In the Druid Zodiac, Aquarius is the sign of the Rowan Tree, the Druidic tree of life. They also referred to it as 'Quickbeam' and it was grown for protection against lightning and witchcraft. Its bright red berries healed the wounded and was described as the 'food of the gods'. The Celts' favourite time for marriage was at the time the Rowan tree shed its fruit, a symbol of fertility and a sacred blessing on the union. The power of the Rowan was also used by the Druids to immobilize the ghosts of the dead by driving Rowan stakes through the heart of the corpse. Rowan wands were used to compel demons to answer difficult questions. This divining aspect of the Rowan is relative to the card, which promotes new hope for the future.

The Star is a radiantly beautiful concept of life and shows the Celtic sense of awe with poetic artistry. It is a card which symbolizes the Garden of Eden restored on earth, a visionary concept of the new Age of Aquarius which could restore man to his rightful place in the universe. On a more personal level, this card deals with restoring the hopes and faith of the querent and opening up a new, as yet unconceivable, horizon. It shows the world to the querent with a new ideal and meaning — a revolutionary ideal which requires a change of attitudes.

When drawn in a spread this card speaks to the individual as no other card can, indicating a time to become more independent and seek one's destiny.

Dignified It brings unexpected help and shows the way ahead is now more promising. If ill-health or a difficult situation exists, the card is quite literally an inspiration, a spiritual tonic. It shows a great calm descending upon the querent which allows him or her to see matters more clearly. It is also associated with a birth of a child if the neighbouring cards concur.

Ill-dignified The querent is easily deceived and some loss or theft of possessions occurs. It can also be a sign of impotence as the querent struggles with life generally. The neighbouring cards would have to be extremely negative for the Star not to operate — any adversities would be a passing phase only.

The Star is a shining light which brings hope, often in the hour of crisis when darkness appears to immobilize all the senses.

The Moon

The two interlocking circles correspond with the two cycles of the Moon: the waxing and waning cycles. The Moon was a Lunar Goddess to the Celts and the Druids called her 'Arianrhod, Lady of the Silver Wheel' — a lady of mystery and magic who stands at both ends of the silver cord of life. Life and death to the Celts was an endless cycle of birth. Death was not a final step, merely a transitional journey. The young Goddess, surrounded by the vibrant colours of life, is holding the symbols of the full Moon and the new Moon, representing the two phases over which she presides — fertility and birth.

The old Goddess is partially veiled, and the ghostly hounds caught up in a wild chase form a circle around her as they blindly pursue their quarry. The two candles are beginning to flicker as life dims. It is a time which creates fear and dread in most mortals. But the Goddess symbolizes the indestructible forces of nature. She covers her face with one arm to hide her vast age, and evokes the lunar energies to return her youth. The two Goddesses are but two phases or faces of the Lunar Goddess. The triple aspect is more complex, an extension of the dual aspect shown in the card.

The young Goddess is really two aspects — Maiden and Mother. The old Goddess is the Matron or Hag. Her cycle is the most mysterious as she presides over the Gateway of the Underworld which leads to death. It was also a path

linked with initiation, a ritual practised by Druids.

As part of their training, they crawled into the ancient burial chambers or barrows to meditate and meet death face to face. The spectre of the Hag was the silent witness, for she speaks not to man. Her presence was a confirmation of the initiation.

The astrological sign of Pisces is associated with The Moon and symbolized by the two fishes swimming in opposite corners at the base. Pisces is a dual sign, known to the Druids as the Ash Tree — a sign associated with the Celtic Triple Goddess and the Sea, over which she also presides. The virtues of the tree were also dual — a sign of life and death. Ash roots were known to strangle those of other forest trees; but the wood was also carved into talismans as a protection against drowning.

The dual aspect of The Moon is symbolic of the highest and lowest elements of nature. The card deals with the same human strengths and weaknesses, also the sexuality of the querent. Whilst it promotes an imagination of the highest order in the arts generally, it is also associated with all the base and lower aspects of character. The darker aspect of The Moon is an amoral force, oblivious to all accepted standards of behaviour. If the neighbouring cards are negative influences, The Moon will indicate the amoral person.

Dignified It shows danger and deception to the querent from outside forces. Hidden enemies or false friends pose a threat to the querent. The intuitive nature is more apparent. A time when uncanny or strange dreams occur, a sense of *déjà vu* exists around the querent. Fateful meetings of a sexual nature also occur and odd experiences generally.

Ill-dignified The emotional nature of the querent is very unstable. The strength and health of the querent is undermined by the current situation, which may mean a period of complete rest. If the querent is a woman, this card can mean problems with the reproductive organs. A time to recuperate and regain strength.

The Moon is an elusive force. Both physically and spiritually it deals with the whole scenario of life and death. It is a sign of the matriarchal energies, good or evil — a force which the querent must come to terms with sooner or later.

The Sun

The Sun rises in the form of Lugh, the Celtic God of Light. With his arms raised above his head, he holds the eternal flame of light — the life of creation. All ancient Sun gods

were associated with the procreation of life. The Sun was the source of light and warmth which fertilized all life on earth. Lugh was a sacrificial Sun god, whose death was celebrated by the Celts with the festival of Lammas on the first of August. It was the traditional time of reaping the harvest, the fruition of life. Before he became a sacrificial god, Lugh was a great warrior, a champion of the Celts in their early battles against other invading tribes. He was known to the Gauls and Irish Celts as 'Lugh the Long-handed'. He possessed a magic spear which flashed fire and roared in a loud voice when used in battle.

As the Celtic race evolved, their religion reached a higher philosophy, the core of which implied the struggle of the soul with the powers of darkness. Druid thought and teaching had reached some astute knowledge and wisdom long before the Romans invaded Britain. By the time Christianity arrived, the seeds had already been sown regarding a sacrificial god. Jesus the new saviour was remarkably like the Gaulish god Hesus, also known to the British Celts as Hu. The Sun was the seat or centre of this divinity, and Hesus occupied a Sun-throne, which was the centre of the Celtic Golden Wheel of Life.

The rising spirit of Lugh, who evolved into Hu, is a significant symbol of the Resurrection of Christ. The woman and two children represent the birth of light and new hope — the birth of Christianity. The message of love and forgiveness was a powerful one. It inspired the early Celtic saints and kings to set new examples of human behaviour. The Holy Grail legend evolved in Britain as a Christian quest, but the Celts had founded the whole Grail myth on the Cauldron of Ceridwen, a symbol of fertility. It reveals the mystical plane at the centre of their religion — a symbol of light represented by the Sun, with Ceridwen — the Guardian of the Cauldron — providing the lunar source of inspiration — the fundamental integration of the male and female principles of life.

This card deals with the integration of the personality

and character. But it is primarily related to the positive aspects of character, the powerful drive of the querent, which could be termed masculine. It also represents the masculine or patriarchal influence of the father, or the male partner, if the querent is female; fatherhood and children if the querent is male. A very positive card to draw if contemplating parenthood. Generally speaking, it is linked to growth and maturity. The sacrificial aspect is the responsibility of the family, which overrides some personal ambitions.

Dignified It shows a personal contentment and material success. For both male and female querents it can signify a successful marriage. It is also a sign of further success and material gains. The creative talents are being fully utilized, promotion and recognition is imminent. All round, a very positive influence prevails.

Ill-dignified The sign of arrogance and vanity, but not a bad card generally. The querent will still be successful, but he or she will have to resist being overly confident and pompous. Some extravagance is the weak point to watch. Overcommitment in financial affairs may occur and caution is advised.

The Sun is a sign of achievement and skilful talents. It shows the strength of a character which has matured.

Judgement

The angel blows the Horn of Gabriel, a symbol of judgement in the Bible. The stairway leads to the centre of the solar disc, and into the redeeming fire of the Creator. The two figures of a man and woman have been summoned by the angel and reverently await their fate. The judgement scene of the dead or departed souls is the

Celtic vision of judgement — after their conversion to
Christianity. It shows an acceptance of their fate, an
acknowledgement of a higher judgement. In the pre-
Christian age, the Celts believed man could descend into
the Underworld or 'Annwn' (an astral plane) not only for
the purpose of subduing its evil inhabitants, but also to
learn their secrets, thus freeing them for their journey into
their heaven, the 'Land of Youth'.

The Druids were the administrators of the public or
social law of the Celtic people. They were also the arbi-
trators of disputes amongst the various tribes. Although
their power was absolute, all men and women could speak
in their own defence and demand certain rights — an
extraordinary democratic procedure in a pagan world.
Their belief in the immortality of the soul meant that a
judgement made in this world was binding in the next

incarnation — even debts of money were apparently transferrable. The old saying 'live now, pay later' is perhaps a significant reminder, an echo of Druidic thought and philosophy.

The element of Fire — the Fire of redemption or retribution — is traditionally associated with the card of Judgement. In the Druid Zodiac of Sacred Trees, the element of Fire is attributed to the Alder Tree, the sign of Aries. The Alder became a symbol of resurrection in 'The Battle of the Trees'. It was a saga of spiritual conflict, fought by the Druids to maintain their ancient order and intellectual superiority over the increasing numbers of invaders of the British Isles. The buds of the Alder are set in a spiral, the symbol of evolution both upwards or downwards. The Celts believed that wicked or evil people would quite literally change into the meanest worm which had consumed their body. They would then have to evolve all over again.

This card deals with a stage of personal development. A climactic crossroads has been reached which can be good or bad. Some kind of assessment or judgement is necessary in order to define the boundaries. The Celts believed in three circles of existence or boundaries; the all-enclosing circle of God alone — Ceugant; the circle of Gwynvydd, the abode of good men and women who have passed through their terrestrial changes; the circle of Abred or Evil, a cycle through which all of mankind must pass before being qualified to enter the circle of Gwynvydd. The querent's stage of development might not be as dramatic, but an issue or matter must be settled to allow a future cycle to proceed.

Dignified A time of personal choice or being able to make an important decision unhindered. A change of position often means a new residence or a totally new career. A final decision is made which is singularly crucial to the querent and will fall in his or her favour. It indicates a time to put one's house in order and settle outstanding debts.

Ill-dignified Decisions go against the querent. Loss through a lawsuit or a legal matter binds the querent to make amends, i.e. fines or having to sell personal possessions to settle claims. A lack of faith in the religious or ethical sense: an unsettling time all around.

The card of Judgement is an arbitrator of natural justice. Although it does relate to legal and material matters, it is primarily concerned with exposing injustices.

The World

The Celtic Wheel of Life is unveiled. The Fool has completed his journey and occupies the Circle of Gwynvydd, a point of realization which the Celts identified as having reached a state of freedom in human form. The struggle of life has been momentarily halted. The four Celtic symbols of the elements which control the world or universe are in abeyance. They look up towards The Fool, who represents the querent and his quest for knowledge — the type of knowledge bound with wisdom of a visionary nature.

The intricate tapestry of life is shown in the colour vibration of the card. The Celts were remarkable visionaries as is revealed in their mystical art and sense of destiny. Their conversion to Christianity was well timed. The Druidic philosophy and religion that had previously stimulated their lives became regenerated into the Christian cause.

The Fool is holding the symbols of earthly power and wearing the purple robe of spiritual adepthood. The four elements of Air, Fire, Earth, Water are portrayed by four curious figures: the bearded half-man, the fiery lion, the gentle calf, the bird-like reptile. They represent the

mystical phases of development, the successive meta-
morphoses of man. There are many references to this state
of being which are found in the bardic poems and songs of
the Celts. The most complete version is 'The Song of
Amergin' which describes the origins of Man, the
Universe, the Creator. It is the Celtic equivalent to the
Book of Genesis but in a literary style more akin to the
hearts and minds of Celtic people, past and present.

The planet Saturn is traditionally associated with this
card. The Druids called this planet Sadorn and it represented certain restrictions. Man was bound to the Celtic
Wheel of Life, his free will was devised to fulfil his
obligations. The Birch Tree in the Druid Zodiac was associated with Sadorn, who became Satan in the Christianized
version of the struggle of the soul. The Devil or Satan does
reflect the harsh nature of Sadorn, but the whole idea of

confrontation with the Devil was to purge the soul to make it stronger, not to destroy it. The association of Saturn with this card has the same implications.

This card deals with the ability to transcend the situation at hand. The previous card of Judgement has already paved the way. The querent has finally reached a point of recompense or reward. It may mean a complete new lifestyle, not just another cycle. The neighbouring cards will either limit or extend the opportunities, but a successful period is indicated. The whole significance of the card has much higher and deeper philosophical implications and should not be interpreted in mundane terms alone.

Dignified It shows a new environment. The querent may be contemplating emigration to another country. Travel and the expansion of one's horizons becomes a reality and not a dream. Frustrating restrictions are removed. The querent recognizes his or her own strength of purpose, which is the directive of this card.

Ill-dignified The querent is still hesitant and inclined to change his or her mind. The whole situation will stagnate if the querent does not act quickly. An opportunity has occurred which must be seized or the querent may live to regret it.

The World is a catalyst to expansion, but within the defined limits of the querent. These limits are, however, much wider and more compensating than the querent may realize.

The Minor Arcana

The Minor Arcana of 56 cards is further divided into four parts or suits. They are based on the four elements of Fire, Water, Air, Earth, symbolized by Wands, Cups, Swords, Coins. Each suit has 14 cards beginning with the Ace — Ten numerically, plus four Court cards. The Court cards represent the personal characteristics and controlling factors. When drawn in a spread they indicate a person who is involved in the situation and will try to influence an outcome. The Court cards also represent energies which can be non-personal or relate entirely to the querent. For example, Pages can be the messengers of situations rather than actual people, and Knights can indicate the active intelligence of the querent. The Queens can emphasize the enduring qualities and the Kings the most original.

The numbered cards are the intentions, actions, thoughts, emotions which create changes. They are, however, manipulated by both the Major Arcana and Court cards. Their action is the lifeblood or force of energy which permeates Nature, Mankind and the Universe. The Court cards have been listed for quick reference to the mythological Celtic characters used to describe the cards.

Cards	Celtic Character
King of Wands	The Spirit of King Arthur
Queen of Wands	Young Queen Boudicca
Knight of Wands	Sir Percival, Knight of the Round Table
Page of Wands	Irish Herald

King of Cups	King Meliodas of Lyonnesse
Queen of Cups	Queen Elizabeth of Lyonnesse
Knight of Cups	Sir Galahad, Knight of the Round Table
Page of Cups	Young Sir Tristan of Lyonnesse
King of Swords	King Uriens of Gore
Queen of Swords	Queen Morgan le Fay of Gore
Knight of Swords	Sir Balin, Knight of Two Swords
Page of Swords	Young Sir Gawaine of Orkney
King of Coins	King Lot of Orkney
Queen of Coins	Queen Margawse of Orkney
Knight of Coins	Sir Bors, Knight of the Round Table
Page of Coins	Young Celtic Scholar

WANDS

The Wand is a symbol of the Spirit of Primal Fire, the mystical symbol which awakens the spiritual will of man. Fire is the element traditionally associated with Wands. Wands have also been called Rods and Staffs, but for divining purposes, Wands is preferable as it conveys the idea of initiating changes which are mysterious or magical. Wands were carried by Druids as symbols of their authority and power. The wands were made from the twigs and slender branches of the trees sacred to the Druids.

A Druidical wand with a spiral decoration similar to the wand depicted on the card was found in Anglesey, and dated around the first century AD. It was made of ash, but the Druids also used rowan, birch, and alder. Each had a peculiar virtue and they were used for various rituals. The birch wand was used for expelling evil spirits; the alder was a Fire symbol of resurrection; the rowan compelled demons to answer difficult riddles. White-hazel wands were carried by Irish heralds as a symbol of arbitration and wisdom. A great many more could be listed, but the oak wand was perhaps the most sacred of all and the word 'Druid' in Welsh is Derwydd or Oak-seer.

The oak tree was also associated with their Sun-gods, the sacrificial gods who were later identified with Jesus and King Arthur of Cornwall. This design of Wands is also shown with the powerful solar-phallic symbol of Fire, a sign of resurrection and the illumination of the spirit.

In 'The Song of Amergin' an ancient poem chanted by Irish bards to convey the wisdom of God, there is a reference to Fire which speaks thus: 'I am a battle-waging spear, I am a god who forms fire for a head.' It symbolizes the idea of Fire as the means of formulating the will of God. Wands convey the energy of Fire in a 'battle-waging spear' a force which strikes a lightning flash of spiritual wisdom.

The purple and violet spirals which form the borders on the suit of Wands are the symbolic colours of the spiritual and divine energies operating. In more mundane terms, the Wands represent the enterprising qualities in man that are actively engaged. The deeper significance shows an awakened spiritual will which creates subtle changes of character — the mysterious and magical action of Wands.

Ace of Wands

The design and symbolism of Wands show a dramatic forceful impact, and the Ace is the most dynamic. The element of Fire is the radiating force and represents the primary energy of the universe. The wand shown in the card had symbolically split the energy of the Sun, a spontaneous action similar to nuclear fission caused by the splitting of an atomic nucleus. The result is an outpouring or release of energy. The card signifies a force which is released rather than invoked (as would be the case with the Ace of Swords).

The impulse of the Ace of Wands initiates the start of a new enterprise. It is also related to birth and the origins of the family. A powerful card to draw at any time, it symbolizes all the creative and inventive qualities which enable mankind to progress. The Ace of Wands conducts energy with great skill and enterprise.

Dignified It shows great initiative and enterprise; high ambitions which may appear beyond the scope of others; revelations of a spiritual nature that act like a catalyst to the understanding of much wider issues.

Ill-dignified Blind optimism with a tendency to create

over-elaborate schemes or plans. The action of the querent becomes extreme and exhaustive. Excessive behaviour generally and a lack of tact or diplomacy.

Two of Wands

The two wands stand like two pillars to a gateway, which leads to the discovery of riches and fame. The Sun is symbolically linked to reaping a harvest, an action of cutting down one life to provide another form of life. Such is the action of the card, which means some sacrifices need to be made in order to make any headway or gain. The initial aggression which creates opposition can also provide some useful co-operation at a later date.

There is a need for independence and a certain freedom of action which can place the querent on a solo path for a while. But the numerical significance of two is also an indication of another person or partner involved somewhere behind the scenes. The traditional explanation is a temporary division or separation with no marriage possible at this time.

Dignified Bold schemes and ventures which may mean travel and separation from partner. The dominant influence of another, whilst beneficial, can restrict the freedom of the querent, or vice versa.

Ill-dignified Some loss or sadness, but a change of circumstances is imminent. The acquisition of wealth has brought a sense of loneliness or isolation.

Three of Wands

The three wands are placed across each other to form a greater strength for a singular purpose. There is a sense of co-operation found in this card which creates more opportunities and the extension of business enterprises. More communication generally shows extra mail and the need to instruct others — a hectic period of activity and some struggles, but with a successful result or conclusion.

The negative aspect of the card shows a sense of pride which can become a stumbling block. It can turn to conceit and the pursuit of superficial values or success. A fast-moving influence overall.

Dignified A progressive period, but not much time to enjoy success. A sense of personal achievement, although help from others has opened the doors.

Ill-dignified Some unexpected disappointments. Friends

or colleagues are less co-operative. A situation of mixed loyalties on both sides.

Four of Wands

The four wands are resting on each other and form a diamond-shaped archway. The Sun is sinking slowly below the horizon, a symbol of rest and repose. A peaceful scene that indicates the completion of the matter; the gathering of the family after a separation or argument; time to celebrate and enjoy the fruits of labour.

A good card to draw if a family dispute exists, a happy conclusion generally. Activity around the home is a major factor, which suggests improvements or new furnishings. But the social life is limited as family matters dominate.

Dignified The satisfaction of a job well done. A cause for celebration in the family. If house-hunting, the ideal home becomes available. A quiet period spent at home or in a favourite retreat.

Ill-dignified Uncertain conditions and conclusions. Not a bad card generally, the neighbouring cards will determine the extent of the disruption caused.

Five of Wands

The five wands appear to be entangled in some kind of dispute with the fifth wand pointing towards the querent in an aggressive manner. But it is a card which signifies life itself, a potent energy of display rather than a serious conflict. The querent might very well be involved in all sorts of activities which conflict with each other — perhaps a clash of personal ambitions.

Life can become a series of confrontations and intricate

manoeuvres. The thrust of this card, however, often forces the issues which have become stagnant or muddled. But it also indicates rash moves due to frustration. The action of the card is directed towards breaking out of an imposed limit or restriction. It may also be linked to sexual frustration.

Dignified The querent will overcome the current obstacles after a period of struggle. The courage of the querent shows strength of character and great resolve, magnanimity even in defeat.

Ill-dignified A dispute is escalated and becomes violent and bitter. All the negative aspects of character, which are arrogant and base, surface.

Six of Wands

The six wands form a harmonious pattern of balance and strength. The solar flames resemble the golden petals of a sunflower as they entwine with the wands. This is a card of gain and victory. The victory is well-earned after a period of strife and hardship. It has several aspects, which range from the arrival of good news to even greater expectations. There is no limit to the success which perhaps best describes this card.

Life is very pleasant and news from distant lands may prompt travel and the seeking of new horizons generally. The search for a deeper philosophy of life may also occur. The positive action of Fire is conducted with great flair and a certain amount of theatre or drama.

Dignified Public recognition and acclaim. News and messages from abroad. A time to celebrate and offer the olive branch to past adversaries. A positive hope for the future.

Ill-dignified Some apprehension or uncertainty regarding the conciliatory actions of recent adversaries. A sense of unease, which requires some frank and honest exchanges.

Seven of Wands

The six crossed wands are held in check by one central wand. This card symbolizes courage and strength, but the outcome of a current crisis is uncertain. It depends entirely on the personal integrity and unwavering courage of the querent. However, the querent or the person concerned has already shown a certain amount of courage by tackling the problem in the first place. The odds may be against the querent, but his or her best line of defence is to attack the antagonist at every opportunity.

It shows fierce competition in the business world, stiff opposition and sharp practice. Any negotiations are difficult to arrange. The dispute may be over a matter which has grown out of all proportion and which involves personal pride. The neighbouring cards will decide the outcome, but the courage is undisputed.

Dignified Unfair competition, but there is a chance of reversing the situation by using a superior strategy. Certain proposals are being considered, but under pressure.

Ill-dignified The querent is forced to give way on some important issues. Not a compromise, but a definite sense of loss at being cheated.

Eight of Wands

The eight wands balance each other into two sets of four. The wands point in two directions — towards and away from the querent. The solar symbol in the centre has four curled flames, which further extend the area of activity. It appears that all the wands are on the move like flaming spears, which reflect the action of the card: speedy transactions or communications, that may be linked to a new writing talent.

The card also deals with the hopes and promises lovers make. If awaiting such news, a speedy conclusion or an announcement is imminent. It also signifies that the matter is now out in the open and no longer concealed. Generally, a card of swift action.

Dignified A broadminded response to a situation. A matter will be swiftly settled which may take the querent by surprise. The querent achieves a new sense of freedom.

Ill-dignified A hasty letter, ill-conceived, causes some anger. Some dishonesty or lack of discretion is brought into the open which could have wider implications or repercussions.

Nine of Wands

The nine wands form a pattern of diamond shapes with the central wand directing the energies with reinforced vigour. The solar system is placed at the base or foundation of the matter to strengthen the whole structure. The card is one of great stamina and powers of recovery. It shows strength in opposition which can be directed for or against the querent. If health has been a source of concern, this card shows a good recovery.

There is a successful outcome indicated, but not without some scars of a previous battle. Some restlessness or unease may still exist, but for the time being there is an obvious advantage. Intellectual pursuits are also related to this card, and a sense of prophecy. The querent may have gained an insight into the nature of mankind and the universe through a series of painful self-examinations.

Dignified Strength of convictions in the face of great opposition. Successful outcomes generally, but only after some setbacks. Recovery from a serious illness.

Ill-dignified Delayed or postponed meetings. The opposition refuses to make contact. Unreasonable terms and bad faith in business and personal matters. A lack of initiative.

Ten of Wands

The ten wands are tightly interwoven into a solid wall of energy and action. The solar symbol burns through the whole structure with great force. This aspect of Fire can be destructive in action and depressive on a spiritual level. The card signifies a success which brings its own burdens. It is an overbearing force which cannot be harmonized.

Whatever is gained at this time has little joy or pleasure. The best that can be said is that the self-sacrifice made is a positive gesture at this time. There is, however, a selfish element attached to the card which cannot be overlooked. Any legal matters or lawsuits will be costly, and the outcome not worth the time and effort spent.

Dignified Money or position gained at this time is well-earned, but lacks a sense of achievement. Someone may take up the cause or responsibilities of the querent but his or her demands are excessive.

Ill-dignified Slander and libel actions against the querent. The opposition is formidable. Treachery and conspiracy from unexpected quarters.

Page of Wands

The Page of Wands is en route with an important message, but he breaks his journey to rest. He sits by a warming fire and gazes into the distant sunset. Two shooting flames rise above him and light up the sky. It symbolizes the light of the illuminated spirit, an uplifting experience. The staff besides him is a hazel wand, a symbol of his authority. Ancient Irish heralds carried white-hazel wands as symbols of arbitration and wisdom. The Page of Wands is a faithful envoy and arbitrator.

If the Page is drawn next to a card representing a male,

it shows a favourable testimony of character. The Page is intelligent, noble and brave. He is the extreme individualist who loves and hates with equal passion. There is also an unpredictable streak and a tendency for rash and impulsive actions. His actions often show a link with inherited skills or family intelligence. The Page is delivering a message to the querent which has great significance for a personal relationship or a private enterprise.

Dignified Good news which brings great joy and comfort. A young man who helps the querent settle a difficult problem. A young person in the family who is now more settled and contented.

Ill-dignified A young ambitious person creates some problems. Bad-mannered and shallow individuals generally.

Knight of Wands

The charging knight on a fiery steed gallops into the picture with great speed and potential violence. The cross on his shield, however, indicates a Holy crusade or quest. His name is Sir Percival de Galis, Knight of the Round Table. During his quest for the Holy Grail he spent many years in distant parts and witnessed some extraordinary phenomena. He had seen The Lion and The Serpent fighting each other with great ferocity, and had instinctively gone to the aid of the young lion, thinking it the more natural beast of the two.

The Lion was the symbolic force or spirit of the new Christian religion. The Serpent represented an older and more ancient wisdom of the Goddess, which became identified with the Devil. Sir Percival was successful in his search for the Grail; his greatest strength was his faith

and love of Christ. The character of the Knight of Wands is intensely loyal and just, although he tends to express his opinions with great force. His great weaknesses are his pride and intolerance. Whilst his courage is never in doubt, if badly dignified a cruel and haughty contempt for others will surface.

Dignified Departure for foreign lands. Prophetic vision and a time of much change and activity. A change of residence or a journey with a stranger who arrives on the scene with great show.

Ill-dignified Prejudice and intolerance. A boastful person who torments others into rash actions. An offensive sense of humour — practical jokes and pranks which misfire.

Queen of Wands

The young woman holds a flaming torch and a wand as she walks through a meadow of sunflowers. Her unadorned golden-red hair falls loosely around her shoulders. The simple robe of pale blue indicates a sign of the neophyte. She is the young Celtic princess destined to become the great warrior Queen Boudicca. But her appearance is more mystical than warlike, as she heads towards the sacred grove to meet with the Druids. She had not sought power, but the Druids have already prophesied her destiny.

Her strength of character is one of calm authority. She knows how to inspire the love of her people and win respect. But there is a brooding side to her nature which is inclined to dwell on personal slights and harbour revenge. When the Romans foolishly scorned her rank and

molested her family her rage became a fury which shook the very foundations of Rome. In her eventual defeat, she took poison rather than submit to humiliation. A proud woman, who could become a tyrant and react with great savagery, yet an immensely kind and loving mother. This is the character of the Queen of Wands.

Dignified A kind and caring woman, someone well-disposed towards the querent. A woman who introduces the querent to some useful and prominent people. An indication of some success in business.

Ill-dignified A dangerous enemy. A woman who was once a friend but has now turned against the querent. It shows stupidity and obstinacy, false pride and snobbery — a furious onslaught which is undeserved.

King of Wands

The King of Wands is a regal monarch, a wise ruler and defender of the weak. His purple cloak signifies his royal status, and the long blue tunic is a symbolic colour of mercy. The book on his knee is securely sealed and signifies the divine law of the universe. He is one of the guardians of knowledge, the non-intellectual kind. He represents the spiritual will, the conscious and deliberate choice of action.

His crown has the symbol of the cross which radiates an unearthly light as he holds the Wand of Fire. Two symbols of energy — fire of fire, the most illuminating light of all. Here is King Arthur of Cornwall, the last of the great Celtic kings of Britain. He reappears as the ancient belief of a great hero, not dead but only sleeping. He will return one day to save the nation in the hour of great darkness. He has of course returned many times in the spirit of great enterprise and brave action, which is the spirit and action of the King of Wands.

Dignified A mediator, a strong character with moral integrity. He acts quickly to settle a dispute and supports the querent. His presence may also bring some financial gains or an unexpected inheritance.

Ill-dignified A bigoted and unpredictable character. A warning to the querent to be apprehensive and stay cool in the hour of crisis.

CUPS

The Suit of Cups is represented by a golden chalice, which became identified with the legend of the Holy Grail, a sacred chalice or cup used in the Last Supper by Jesus and brought to Cornwall by Joseph of Arimathea. The cup represented the blood of Christ, the source of all life. The Water element associated with cups was considered by the Celts and many ancient people to be the source of life. Such comparisons show the continuity of spiritual evolution.

In the Tarot, Cups are related to the emotions, the highly sensitive and vulnerable part of human nature. The emotional nature is activated by the intuitive response to a situation, which is the unconscious state of being. The realm of the unconscious self is vast and fluid. It can be briefly reached in dreams and harnessed sometimes through the imagination, a faculty of resourcefulness and inspiration. When the spread contains a number of Cups, the emotional state is obvious, but there is a deeper significance of great sensitivity and self-awareness. The creative talents are also aroused and become productive.

The Water element is traditionally associated with the feminine aspects of nature, the fertile action which can remain passive. Cups is the complement to Wands, the Fire element related to the masculine impulse of action. The word 'passive' appears to signify a line of submission, but it really implies a state of unquestioned faith and obedience to God. The source of life and inspiration is found by the passive action of Cups.

The negativity of Cups, however, can be a state of complete inertia, a dreamlike state that encourages self-deception to the detraction of a situation. The dual nature is also compounded by Cups and relates to personal relationships, the experience of which shows more complicated issues to contend with. Personal relationships are the extension of self-awareness and can create a sense of 'oneness' if the relationship is perfectly balanced. The Holy Grail was the symbolic search for finding a 'oneness' with God or the higher state of being to which man aspires.

Ace of Cups

The Celtic Cross symbolizes the early Christian faith which inspired the Holy Crusades and the legend of the Holy Grail. The Grail was a sacred chalice, a symbol of life and the divinity of Christ. The chalice became the focus of much speculation and romantic imagination. The Ace of Cups is a symbol of the divine consciousness of God, which can be reached. The card also represents the element of Water in its most sacred and original form. The fertility and productivity associated with Water is both spiritual and creative. It evokes the intuitive and psychic energies.

The soft colours in the design show the subtlety of the forces operating. The imagination is itself a very subtle faculty which can raise the consciousness to higher levels. The Ace of Cups also signifies the illumination of the beauty of nature.

Dignified Great joy and contentment. The search for happiness is resolved and a new understanding reached. A

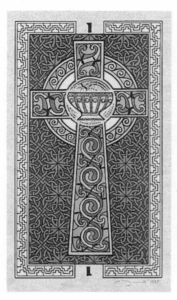 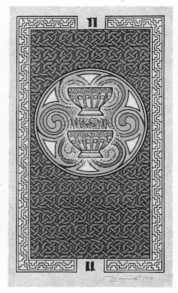

powerful insight into life itself reveals some simple truths. Births in the family.

Ill-dignified Some instability or extreme anxiety. If the neighbouring cards are difficult, this card is a powerful source of light not easily deflected.

Two of Cups

The two cups are placed in a circular window of spirals and form a rose-hexagram. The purple and soft blue colours create a delicate hue, as the amber light shines through the window. This is a card of great affinity and union — a promise made between two people. It is a sign of love and friendship which has a deep significance or commitment.

Marriage is one outcome, but the great rapport shown can also be related to the loving partnership of a married couple.

This is a very powerful attraction of two people that often crosses the dividing line of social and racial barriers. Any personal relationship founded at this time has a chance of lasting happiness.

Dignified Love and marriage. A greater understanding in a partnership. The union of two people which creates a perfect balance of the masculine and feminine qualities.

Ill-dignified An intense relationship which can become too possessive or claustrophobic. Too much time wasted on personal affairs.

Three of Cups

The three cups are placed within three circles. The spiral design in the circles have more colour and movement. The card represents activity and celebration. The pleasures in life tend to dominate the scene. It is a time of abundance and good fortune. A family celebration which helps to heal painful memories. A gathering of people generally to enjoy a special occasion. It may be a musical festival of dancing and singing.

In more personal terms it indicates a time of acceptance or recognizing the virtues of others. Previous distrust may have been well-founded, but the tendency to look backwards must be corrected. The future ahead will become more certain or less complicated if the healing process operates fully. The intuitive nature is extremely sensitive.

Dignified A happy conclusion to any personal problems or family matters. A time of healing which may relate to a previous illness or a personal worry. Generally, a time to celebrate good fortune and good news.

Ill-dignified Some worry or mistrust concerning a present success, which may have occurred too rapidly, or lack real substance.

Four of Cups

The four cups are placed together with an interlocking panel of four circles forming the background. The cups radiate a glow of light with a dazzling quality. Some aspects of the circular design have become obscured or hidden. The card has a similar significance of hidden anxieties. The imagination is overactive and prone to worry. The traditional interpretation is one of blended

pleasure and a certain weariness.

There is, however, some success indicated with this card. Past efforts have secured certain promises which still hold good, but the querent will have to decide on accepting an offer that may undermine the situation. His or her fears may be well-grounded, but it is too easy to jump to the wrong conclusions at this time.

Dignified An offer is made which requires some compromise. Hold on to what has been gained already. If uncertainty does exist, cancel or reject current proposals.

Ill-dignified No progress possible. An uneasy situation restricts the querent at a time when hopes have been falsely raised.

Five of Cups

Four cups are placed upright and one is reversed. It signifies a loss and is another card of blended pleasure — loss and gain. This card, however, is much more disappointing than the four of cups. The reversed cup is a reversal of a situation which stresses the loss rather than any gain which may follow. It shows disappointments in love and is traditionally the card of divorce. If marriage is contemplated, however, it will not be without the frustration of a divorce or bitter regrets.

This sense of bitterness can spoil that which is gained — personal freedom and new start in life. It is linked to inheritances, but once again not without some disappointment. There is a self-destruct mechanism operating which is perhaps the key to understanding this card. The situation has deteriorated through anger and unstable emotions which can be directed against the querent or represent the querent's own feelings.

Dignified Some bitterness and loneliness is experienced, but the way ahead is more clearly defined. The losses are difficult to come to terms with, but the querent may be ignoring all the possibilities.

Ill-dignified Sorrow and a lack of compassion. Circumstances which bring out the worst elements of character by refusing to face up to the facts of life and how to best profit from such a situation.

Six of Cups

The six cups are divided into two sets of three. The triple design has a natural harmony and balance. The card signifies a possible increase, the beginning of a new cycle after a previous loss. There is a reflective aspect and the need to put matters into perspective. In order to look ahead, some reflection on the past will clarify the situation. Memories and old friends often surface together, with unexpected meetings.

This emphasis on a new cycle is the positive aspect of the card and it indicates a new environment and new employment. It is still in the early stages and may not have occured as yet. The card is showing the possibility of change and future success.

Dignified Happiness and the feeling of an inner peace. A love of the simple things in life. Some artistic and often latent talents begin to surface. The support of old friends.

Ill-dignified A tendency to live in the past. A form of self-indulgence exhausts the body. A lack of emotional stamina.

Seven of Cups

Six cups have formed an intricate interlacing pattern at the base of the card and the solarity cup at the top is a reminder of what can be achieved with more single purpose. There is a basic weakness in the card which suggests a corruption of the initial intent or idea. It signifies unfulfilled promises and the deception of illusion. Any attempts made at this time for personal happiness will lack a permanent solution.

What has been achieved in the past must not be discounted, but the querent might be striving for the impossible dream. The present situation requires very careful reassessment.

Dignified A sentimental appraisal of a situation confuses the issues. Not a good time to make important decisions.

Ill-dignified Lustful passions and violent emotions. The querent is being deceived or a form of self-vanity exists. The querent may be looking for a form of escapism through any means available.

Eight of Cups

The eight cups have been further divided and form into two sets of four. In the bottom circle, three cups are upturned to signify an empty feeling of discontent. The decline of the matter is apparent and the card indicates an abandoned dream or success. There is a complete lack of interest in pursuing the matter. The querent is moving away from a situation which has become impossible to handle.

The positive aspect of the card, although limited, does show some small gain by having faced up to the situation. But it is not enough to change anything, hence a departure from the scene. All the cups stacked on top of each other also show the great emotional battle which has gone before.

Dignified The decline of a matter, but the consequences may be less important than first imagined. A search for happiness is the prime motive at this time.

Ill-dignified A restless emotional state and a need to take a vacation. A tendency to disregard the material achievements.

Nine of Cups

The nine cups form three pyramids of perfect balance and harmony. The golden light shines through the circular windows and has filled all the cups with the Holy Water of the Spirit. The card signifies all wishes fulfilled and the realization of true wisdom. In general terms it shows a satisfactory conclusion or outcome of the matter. A feeling of well-being permeates the card and represents the flow of consciousness.

The querent or person concerned is experiencing a great wave of pleasure and happiness. Complete success is hard to visualize, but this card is touching on the secret of perfect happiness which is spiritual and not material. Therefore the wishes fulfilled are the hopes and dreams of a personal nature and do not relate to others at this time.

Dignified Pleasure and complete success. The querent has the advantage in all matters. A kind and generous response to people less fortunate. A sense of destiny is a powerful influence.

Ill-dignified The smug satisfaction of winning shows conceit and a lack of humility. A vain person who only talks about his or her own achievements.

Ten of Cups

The ten cups are interlocked with each other to form a series of individual patterns which make up one complete design. This is a card of success which has a final conclusion and involves the whole family. The individual commitment takes into account a need for others. It is a card of profound love and the joy of giving. A powerful card to draw and one that is not easily displaced.

It is also a card of victory as it disperses the element of Water into a fountain of energy, which fills all the cups in

equal measure. The circuit becomes complete and the emotional nature is stabilized. The Holy Grail is within reach.

Dignified Inspired love and happiness. All personal matters are finally settled and agreed without recriminations. A time for healing others and serving the community.

Ill-dignified False illusions and promises. A waste of natural resources. Not a bad card generally, but the excess of the card can encourage a weak character to react badly.

Page of Cups

The Page of Cups is playing a harp, white doves flutter around him. He is wearing a green cloak, the symbolic colour of fertile earth. The Page represents the earthy part of the Water element. Earth and Water combined shows the faculty of expression which is artistically creative. One dove perches on the chalice to take a drink and the silver light reflects the association with the Holy Grail.

The Page is the young Sir Tristan, the son of King Meliodas of the legendary land of Lyonnesse, which became submerged beneath the sea off the Scilly Islands. His name means 'a sorrowful birth' — given to him by his mother, Queen Elizabeth, who died shortly after his birth. He was a gifted child, both scholarly and musical. He played the harp with unsurpassed skill and sensitivity. His adventures are too numerous to mention, but he was the same brave knight whose love affair with Queen Iseult ended so tragically.

Dignified A studious youth, artistic and gentle. There is a reflective and meditative quality of character that can be courageous when inspired. It also relates to news and

messages, proposals of love and marriage.

Ill-dignified Seductive proposals and ill-founded rumours. Can be lazy or inclined to idle dreams of fancy. A melancholy person who wanders aimlessly.

Knight of Cups

The Knight of Cups stares impassively into another world, as he clasps the sacred chalice of the Holy Grail. The solitary star shines above him and symbolizes the Star of Bethlehem. He had followed the same star to find Christ, but the quest of the Holy Grail was the mystical union with Christ. Christ's blood, said to be held in the sacred chalice, is a symbol of the Holy Spirit.

The Knight is Sir Galahad, the most perfect knight in the world. He was also the greatest knight of all who fought all-comers to win the right to find the Grail. His calm and gentle manner belied his intense and passionate nature. His character was intensely secretive and insular. He was an artist above all else, creating the perfect image of a knight. The character of the Knight of Cups is capable of inspiring both love and fear. A card of great imagination and power.

Dignified The approach of a messenger or lover whose quiet manner does not reflect the nature of things. There is an intensity of secret passion and incitement. It also shows great imagination and vision.

Ill-dignified A subtle person who will cleverly deceive the querent. A person who is ruthless, but inspires devotion.

Queen of Cups

The Queen is filling a cup with water as an act of hospitality and service. Two other cups are placed upon the table, carved in a traditional zoomorphic design of Celtic origin. She is expecting visitors and is preparing some refreshment. The Queen of Cups represents the patient type of woman; her guests have not arrived, but she will make sure that everything is ready for them. Her image is one of tranquillity and infinite subtlety. She has the rare kind of serene beauty and typifies the perfect wife and mother.

Queen Elizabeth of Lyonnesse, mother of Tristan, had these rare qualities. She was a faithful, loving wife, and as she lay dying from the labour of childbirth, she charged her maid to remind the King of her love for him. Her message was also one of love for their son, for whom she requested a Christian baptism. Such is the character of the Queen of Cups — not always physically strong, but a

steady, resolute person when opposed.

Dignified A loving and devoted mother. Someone with vision and a practical wisdom. A kind and sympathetic woman who makes the ideal partner and an honest friend. She will render a service to the querent.

Ill-dignified A woman who is popular, but her appearance may be deceptive. Her expression of feelings may be false or shallow. A dreamy type of character who cannot be relied upon.

King of Cups

The King of Cups sits on a splendid throne surrounded by water. He reflects a passive but creative intelligence. He has an extremely amiable and pleasant nature, at least on the surface. The card represents the fiery part of Water which can signify a swift and passionate attack on the unsuspecting. Fire is an aggressive action, but directed through the Water element of character it is hard to sustain — the passionate attack is limited to bursts of both anger or enthusiasm, but usually non-violent.

King Meliodas of Lyonnesse was such a character. He was kind and placid, but too easily influenced. When he remarried after losing his first wife in childbirth, he chose badly. The new Queen was determined to poison Tristan, his son, so that her own children could inherit. By a stroke of fate she was caught in the act and was ordered by the King to be burnt alive. Tristan pleaded for her life, and she was spared and eventually forgiven by the King.

Dignified A man well-disposed towards the querent. A good businessman, but he can lack the endurance to finish work or settle accounts. He is often religious and susceptible to external forces.

Ill-dignified A sensual man who gives way to his weaknesses. An idle or complacent man who promises more than he can deliver. If drawn with the Nine or Ten of Swords, signs of schizophrenia and instability.

SWORDS

The sword is a weapon of destruction and defence. The symbolism of Swords when used in the Tarot has the same dual purpose. Swords represent the forces of conflict, but they also disperse the stagnant energies that have created the conflict. The element of Air is attributed to the Suit of Swords, and it has an interesting significance describing the dual purpose with great insight. Air is a dimension of communication which relates to the power of the mind.

Mental confusion is the conflict of Swords and angry words are the cutting edge of Swords. Truth wields the Sword with justice not vengeance, and mercy sheaths the Sword with compassion.

The Celts were fearless warriors and their legends contain many references to magical weapons, the most famous being the sword of King Arthur, Excalibur. The story is well known, but the sword was rendered impotent when its scabbard was stolen by the King's half-sister, Morgan le Fay. Possession of the scabbard prevented any wounds being inflicted on the King. The scabbard was also the dual energy that controlled the sword with the application of wisdom.

Swords are drawn when conflict has arisen, but the healing action of Swords can also bring into the open the ill-feelings and negative thoughts which are less harmful — when spoken. The healing aspect of Swords is perhaps often overlooked. When Jesus said 'I have come to bring a sword, not peace' it shocked his disciples. It was, however, a paradox to the message of Christianity — 'The truth will set you free' — the sword being the symbol of truth.

Swords portray the penetrating force of the mind which seeks truth above all other virtues. If the spread contains a number of Swords, a tense situation has developed in the mind of the querent. The arguments or disputes are secondary. The neighbouring cards will indicate the source of such conflict. Cups relate to emotional and domestic problems. Coins relate to financial worry. Wands relate to work and ambitions.

Ace of Swords

The Ace of Swords is held in perfect balance in the Celtic Wheel of Life. The pentacle is the scabbard which controls the powerful symbol of life and death. The sword has transformed the five-pointed pentacle into the Star of

David — a symbol of the evolved Man. The intricate Celtic knotwork within the Wheel forms a pattern of energy that symbolizes life. The point of the sword has pierced the Wheel to touch the spiralling energy of the universe. The hilt has formed a crown above the Wheel and symbolizes the hand of the Creator.

The symbolism of this card is one of great force and reckoning. Aces are traditionally associated with the root source of the elements. They are therefore very potent and have the power to invoke or summon the energies which lie dormant. The Ace of Swords has summoned the element of Air. The querent is confronted with the source of his or her own wisdom — or lack of it. The situation is a critical one. Any action requires great control. The mind is finely balanced between two extreme reactions.

Dignified The removal of obstacles. New beginnings are possible now the incentive is increased. The mind is free of negative thoughts. The course of justice triumphs.

Ill-dignified Extreme reactions open up old wounds and prevent healing. Excessive force is used which creates further antagonism. A spiral of destruction and hatred is evident.

Two of Swords

The Two of Swords has formed an interlocking symbol of the forces of conflict held in check. The diamond-shape knotwork is similarly designed to symbolize a concentration of energy. The two points of the swords are touching a forcefield of energy which has created a natural circuit. The Two of Swords is the only card in the Suit of Swords which enforces harmony or an agreement.

There is a form of intimacy with this card that indicates a lot of discussion taking place. The querent is engaged in settling a dispute which has caused a division in the past and great anguish. This is a card of healing, as both parties are able to speak freely and without bitterness. Communication is the key here. It has provided the means of understanding the other person's viewpoint.

Dignified An honourable settlement of a dispute. No victors or losers. The querent has gained a victory, however, because his or her mind has been opened to an opposing or a polarity of thought.

Ill-dignified An uneasy alliance or truce. Some tension still exists, but the querent must face the truth of the situation. Not a time to be petty or disloyal.

Three of Swords

The two crossed swords are surmounted by a third sword and has split a previous alliance. The circle of interlacing shows a complicated situation which has arisen from an intruder or a third party. The intruding sword is pointed towards the heart of the querent when drawn. It signifies tears and sorrow. The dominant sword relates to a dominant character who has suddenly appeared in the life of the querent.

Promises made have not been kept, and deceitful words are the active ingredient in this card. A separation from partner has occurred or is imminent. There is a disruptive force operating which is difficult to deal with. Jealousy or mischief-making is evident. The neighbouring cards will clarify the situation.

Dignified Not a happy card to draw at any time. Even if drawn as a past situation, a residue of sadness still exists. At best it can show honest intent as a result of suffering.

Ill-dignified Strife and discord prevails. Painful experiences and thoughts blot out happier times. The querent either accepts a situation or must do something about it — and quickly.

Four of Swords

The four swords are cleverly interwoven to form a balance of energies once again. The swirling force of light surrounds and intermingles with the swords, a symbol of the Swastika — an ancient hieroglyph of the universal energies activated by God. Four was a perfect number of completion to the Druids who related it to the Four Spirits or the Four Winds of God.

   This card signifies a rest from conflict, a respite rather than a definite truce. A peaceful situation, nevertheless, and a sign of convalescence. The querent has also been involved with other people's troubles and he or she now seeks a private retreat to gather his or her thoughts. There is a positive healing aspect with this card which shows a recovery from a serious illness.

Dignified A peaceful or serene mind after a series of setbacks. The querent may decide to spend more time alone and rediscover his or her own individuality. Quiet pastimes such as reading or meditation.

Ill-dignified The querent may retreat too far and become cut off from people who could help. A period spent alone has an adverse affect, its extent clarified by the neighbouring cards.

Five of Swords

The five swords are drawn, their blades flash with anger and fury. The forcefield which surrounds the swords is uncontrolled rage. The dominant sword once again divides the querent from friends and his or her own powers of reason. Angry words wound, and this card signifies malice and spite. The swords vibrate with violent thoughts and lies. Conflict around the querent has reached a dangerous climax.

There is an air of defeat and loss, hence the uncontrolled anger and fury. But there are no possible victories on either side, only a dismal note of failure. The grievances have been bitter and spiteful, bringing out the worst aspects of character. The mind is in a frenzy of activity, still trying to win the day — by foul means if necessary. There is an

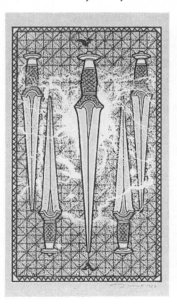 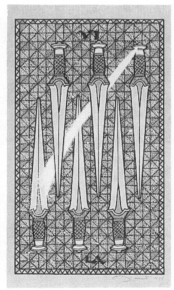

element of grief with this card, however, that does indicate genuine suffering.

Dignified A loss has occurred and has made the querent feel bitter. The cause may have been a just one, but the ensuing conflict has cultivated all the negative cunning of the querent's mind.

Ill-dignified A dangerous rival is intent on causing trouble. Not a time to show pity, which can be mistaken for weakness. Slanderous accusations rebound amongst friends.

Six of Swords

The six swords line up to face each other, and then slot into three dual positions of compromise. A dazzling ray of white light descends from the hilt of the third sword and immobilizes the fourth sword — a sequence of events or movements which now indicates a stronger position all round. The powerful ray of light is a significant symbol of a successful conclusion. It is a success due to tremendous effort, and overcoming many obstacles.

The ray of light reflects the selfless attitude that has prevailed. The previous hardships and strife are no longer relevant. The querent has learned to use the powers of reason with cool efficiency. In the process of overcoming the obstacles, the inventive and highly original part of the brain has been activated. The ray of light was thus switched on. The mind, if properly honed, is sharp as a sword.

Dignified A long holiday is possible now. The life of the querent has reached a certain order after continuous effort. Obligations may still be heavy, but a sense of peace prevails.

Ill-dignified The querent might be going away to forget some disappointments, which is the best move at the present time. The journey itself is perhaps a significant gesture.

Seven of Swords

The seven swords create a brilliant display, but it is an unstable balance of energies which can be undermined. A dominant sword once again disturbs the six interlocking swords. The swirling light has become a powerful current of force and symbolizes nervous tension. The mind becomes strange and brooding. The querent is losing ground at a time when victory is within grasp. The dominant sword symbolizes the intervention of another.

The person in question is intimately concerned with an important project or brainchild of the querent. This person is inclined to offer compliments designed to win confidence or the favour of the querent. The unreliability of this person is not the main threat however. The querent is too easily drawn or distracted through his or her own lapse of judgement. False friends are easily detected if the querent's sense of perspective is working.

Dignified Some success is evident, but more planning is required. It may mean changing the whole structure or framework of the work in hand. A time to make adjustments or more mental notes.

Ill-dignified The opponent has the upper hand. Mental confusion is the result of relaxing at a time of only a partial victory, and someone else may snatch the reward.

Eight of Swords

The eight swords have formed a pattern as intricate as the three knotwork diamond panels which balance the swords. The Celtic Picts had developed the knotwork interlacing with great skill and artistry. It is a geometrical pattern used as a symbol of the continuity of life. The design represents a complicated spiral that forms a maze or labyrinth, and is relative to the card. There is a 'locking in' of energies which places the querent in a restricted position.

The card shows too much attention to detail at the expense of more important matters. The mind becomes a prison of ideas which cannot be readily expressed or exploited. The situation is altogether too intense and claustrophobic. A time when indiscretions will occur, by not thinking of the consequences. Some success in private matters is possible, but it remains an isolated case rather than producing further progress.

Dignified The querent may become involved in short-term projects that lead nowhere in particular, but allow some latitude of thought. A time for reflection, rather than action.

Ill-dignified Malicious thoughts and negative ideas. All news is bad news, as a wave of pessimism sweeps over the querent. A feeling of being trapped — an inability to free oneself from a hopeless situation.

Nine of Swords

The ladder of eight swords is crossed by the ninth sword to form a network of steel. The dominant ninth sword has a pointed sharpness and has pierced a vital life-source. The swords display all the jagged edges of mental cruelty, pain and despair. This is a card of self-inflicted misery, a suicidal frame of mind. The balance of the mind is greatly disturbed. Such suffering can also be the result of malicious gossip.

Too much talk generally has become a negative force. The situation is very critical and will create health problems through the build up of nervous tension. Accidents and miscarriages are related to this card. The agony of the mind is the result of such experiences. Nothing good can be said, so hopefully the neighbouring cards will reduce some of the depressing aspects. Very positive Major Arcana cards would help.

Dignified Passive resistance is required to overcome the current crisis. Any attempt to respond with force or dishonesty will escalate the situation into further despair and suffering.

Ill-dignified The querent is experiencing a very dark period of depression and misery. Resistance to disease is poor, and ill-health is evident. He or she is further burdened with guilt and anguish.

Ten of Swords

All the swords are drawn and present a cutting edge of great destruction. The interlacing of the swords disguises their intent. Whereas the Nine of Swords indicated self-inflicted misery, the Ten of Swords shows the knife in the back. A deadly array of weaponry is at the disposal of enemies. The querent has unwittingly walked into a carefully-laid trap. Destruction is near at hand, but not necessarily a physical death.

It may mean the complete failure of plans, but the mind of the querent suddenly becomes particularly sharp and articulate. This 'cleverness' has, however, been the result of his or her downfall. Undisciplined thought is the most destructive element at the disposal of mankind. The Ten of Swords is a symbol of a spent force, which means the destructive element has reached a peak or climax. Dreadful though the consequences can be, the querent may at last be facing a fundamental truth about him or herself.

Dignified A failure of some kind cannot be avoided, but the extent will rest entirely on the neighbouring cards. A sadness is felt which cannot be removed or forgotten for some time to come.

Ill-dignified A disastrous situation which will mean ruin and great hardship. A violent incident will occur — death, if shown with the Knight of Swords. A breakdown of all communication has occurred.

Page of Swords

The Page of Swords moves stealthily through the forest. His action is silent for he is engaged in a spying mission. The element of cunning is his weapon — no need to draw his sword. One of the aspects of the card is watching the opposition. There is also an angry aspect to the Page — a liking for revenge. Sir Gawaine of the Round Table was a vengeful young man, who was largely responsible for the break-up of the Order by pursuing a furious vendetta against Sir Lancelot. Such extremes reveal the fanaticism of the card.

The Page is traditionally regarded as the 'earthly' part of Air and it shows fixed opinions, which can become powerful negative traits. The action of the card does have a practical application, however; the Page is also quite adept at settling controversial matters with great subtlety.

Dignified It signifies grace and dexterity, a strength of mind which can have a certain wisdom. Also an astute ability for observation and devotion to duty.

Ill-dignified The mind resorts to cunning and cruelty. An underhandedness creates violent reprisals. Sudden, unexpected bad news; or an angry silence prevails.

Knight of Swords

The Knight of Swords is sitting on a windswept mountain,

as the black crows of death hover above him. He clasps the hilt of his sword firmly with one hand as the point pierces the earth. In his other hand he holds some flowers, a symbol of peace and victory, but not without bloodshed. In King Arthur's court, a knight called Balin performed two remarkable deeds in one day. He drew from a magical scabbard a sword which could only be drawn by a knight without treachery or treason — a virtuous, good knight. He then cut off the head of the Lady of the Lake as she arrived to demand her gift from King Arthur for giving him Excalibur. Balin justified his action by claiming the Lady of the Lake was a sorceress who had destroyed both his mother and many good knights.

The Knight is the most potently dangerous force of Air, and the action of this card is to destroy something before it can be established whether it ought to be destroyed. Balin later killed his own twin brother, Balan, by a tragic error of judgement. The inscription on his tomb summarizes the essence of the card: 'The Knight with two swords, he that smote the dolorous stroke.'

Dignified An intense intellect. A formidable opponent or antagonist. Can be a fanatical friend whose loyalty is unquestionable, but whose actions and ideas are not practical.

Ill-dignified Clever deception — a glib tongue. A destructive force is unleashed which can cause ruin, even death, if the neighbouring cards are also fatal influences, e.g. The Devil or the Ten of Swords.

Queen of Swords

The Queen of Swords sits quietly in a forest glade. She is holding a sword in her lap, her right hand clasps the sharp blade to symbolize her passive control. She represents the watery element of Air and her title is the Liberator of the

Mind. The Queen is the subtle interpreter and intense individual. Her whole movement is graceful with a perfected sense of rhythm and balance. These excellent qualities, however, cannot tolerate interference and she can remain aloof and isolated in her own world. Her darker side can be very dangerous, but she does inspire intense love and devotion from the most unexpected sources.

Queen Morgan le Fay was such a person; her character was both devious and yet extremely attractive and enchanting. She managed to deceive King Arthur, her half-brother, whom she had secretly hated for many years. The power of Merlin had prevented her revenge on many occasions. Eventually, she imprisoned Merlin with the aid of Vivien, one of the young Ladies of the Lake, and set in motion Arthur's decline and death.

Dignified A clever, but scheming woman. The card also represents a keen perception, with the ability to act swiftly.

Ill-dignified A sign of separation, and the sterility or barrenness associated with widowhood and female sadness. A sharp-tongued woman causes pain and much sorrow.

King of Swords

The King of Swords holds his sword clasped in front of him and rests his arms on his shield. The pose is one of self-confidence. His penetrating eyes reveal his commanding presence as he gazes intently towards the querent. He represents the fiery part of Air, an element of dynamic energy and brilliant intellect. He is a decisive character, someone who will have initiative and authority; not a person to offend at any time, and whose superior intelligence restricts intimacy of any kind. Such a character responds well in emergencies and can immediately gauge the situation, often acting with incredible speed and bravery.

King Uriens of Gore was the husband of Morgan le Fay. He became a loyal friend to King Arthur and managed to survive several attempts on his life which had been instigated by his wife. But he was a lonely king who could not inspire the love of his wife, illustrating the aspect of the card which is one of isolation and mistrust.

Dignified It shows a militant intelligence and the support of great force. It has an impartial but cold judgement. A fierce friend who has courage; someone who is subtle and clever in action.

Ill-dignified A person who becomes a tyrant and forces the

issues. The mind becomes cruel and sly, but not without severe suffering. A tortured mind under a calm exterior.

COINS

The symbol of Coins represents the material world. A coin is a metal disc, a medium of exchange for material possessions. Long before banknotes became a legal currency, coins were the symbol of wealth and power. Some of the earliest known coins in Britain were made of gold and were of Greek origin. The Celts were skilled metalworkers, and when they started to mint their own coins around the first century BC they copied the Greek designs of figureheads, horses and chariots. Later on, they began to develop their own styles and symbols, but they continued to use the symbol of the Wheel which represented part of the chariot. The Wheel evolved into an important Celtic symbol of life.

The Suit of Coins in the Celtic Tarot are Wheel symbols of the continuity of life, shown with the gold interlacing knotwork. Gold was the Celts' favourite metal and was used for coins and jewellery. The design on all the cards has a green background of spirals representing the energies of Earth, the element of Coins. Wealth was often associated with the dark gods of the Underworld in Celtic mythology. The precious metals were dug out of the earth, and the mine shafts became the entrances or gateways to the Underworld. The Cornish tin-miners observed the custom of leaving some of their food for the 'Bockles or Knockers' the earth piskies or spirits who watched them. Failure to do so was to risk a cave-in or, worse, a loss of life.

But the God of the Underworld has always exacted a price for his treasure. Money has been called the 'root of all evil'; it signifies a power source which can create greed and corruption. The Suit of Coins, like Swords, has a dual action of both good and evil. The division of wealth creates two societies — the rich and the poor.

The Celts were not materialistic by nature; they placed the arts above all else — a *cultural* wealth was their heritage. They had already established a profound belief in the immortality of the soul that displaced the power of wealth. The Romans were amazed at the Celtic custom of not looting the dead on the battlefields. The Celts would often take the possessions of the dead, particularly the fine weapons, and throw them into the nearest stream or river. Whilst they feared the ghosts of the dead, they feared the God of the Underworld even more. Throwing the weapons away was seen as an act of returning property to the rightful owner.

This particular aspect of their character is a significant introduction to Coins. When interpreting the symbolism of the Tarot it is important to remember that Coins represent material gains and losses which do not necessarily mean good fortune or unhappiness. In fact they often show a need to respect the true values of life.

Ace of Coins

The Ace of Coins has one circular panel of knotwork with an interlacing border which joins up the whole design of the card to represent the energies of earth in continuous motion. It is an intricate design and symbolizes all the material senses. The force and energy contained in the card are powerful, but the card also has a sense of illusion. Its centre remains an isolated force; success — good or bad — lacks a spiritual dimension. Material gain may be sufficient at the time, but it can result in a void of feelings and emotions.

The card does however signify a successful application of labour. It is a creative energy which encourages speculation and a concentration of effort. Aces are always symbols of new beginnings and brighter prospects that set a new pace of life. The querent's personal sense of values may not be materially inclined, but this card does indicate that something of worth or merit is possible. The symbol of Coins, although directly associated with wealth, is also related to a personal recognition of power or authority.

Dignified A fulfilment of desires, which can be related to the birth of a child or a profitable financial speculation. Something of great personal value is promoted or recognized.

Ill-dignified Opulence and a great show of wealth. Too much emphasis on the material assets creates a lack of propriety. The division of wealth becomes unfair.

Two of Coins

An equal balance is restored in the Two of Coins. The two centre panels of knotwork link up to show a certain harmony, but there remains a sense of change or divided assets. The duality of the energies forms two distinct possibilities: gain and loss in equal measure. The card has the potential for both, which also suggests an alternating cycle rather than a definite division. A period quite literally of balancing the books or finances.

The strength and weaknesses of character revolve like two spinning coins — heads or tails. A question mark of intent or purpose. The querent can become industrious or unreliable depending on which way the coins land. There is a sense of risk or chance that adds an element of luck and relates to the planet Jupiter in the astrological division associated with the card. Travel is also indicated and linked to a possible business partnership.

Dignified A pleasant change of scenery. Careful

management of resources. Good news concerning finances. Negotiations for a settlement of money or assets, is fairly divided.

Ill-dignified An inconsistent effort reflects a lack of will-power. The querent tends to wander aimlessly, being too easily distracted. A need to resolve some financial debts.

Three of Coins

The three circular panels of knotwork have become more compact and solid, which relates to the significance of the card. The Three of Coins is traditionally associated with the constructive use of labour and the employment of all resources. The creation of such work demands skilled labour or expertise.

The centralized application of energy shown in this card relates to success and fame — a public recognition of personal skills. The querent may also be involved in a project which requires a retraining programme, a need to utilize all his or her resources and self-discipline. It is also an indication of employment rather than self-employment, of being hired to provide some specialist skills. In more mundane terms it is often associated with repairs or renovations around the home.

Dignified Commercial ventures and the application of skills. The influence of the querent is increased, and shows a rewarding experience which can be a personal satisfaction rather than a financial gain.

Ill-dignified Grandiose plans which lack detail. The inability to delegate work efficiently undermines the situation. Waste and incompetence generally.

Four of Coins

The four coins of knotwork form a cross of balancing energies, united with an oblong border of interlacing. It symbolizes a unity and security which relates to the card. All the energies are carefully distributed and set in motion a material gain. This card is totally materialistic and shows the acquisition of earthly power through wealth.

It is not necessarily a selfish distribution, but the emphasis on acquiring wealth is one of suspicion or feeling insecure. It may take the form of an extravagant gift which makes the querent feel very contented or assured of his or her position. If love is measured thus, the gift is a token of some value, but it will not lead to anything further. There is a limit to personal commitment, perhaps on both sides.

Dignified Financial gain in the form of legacies or personal gifts. It may also mean an early retirement with a 'golden handshake'. The querent is financially secure, but in an isolated position.

Ill-dignified Material possessions are coveted. The power of wealth corrupts and provokes opposition. It can mean debt, but only as a temporary embarrassment.

Five of Coins

The five coins form an elaborate pattern and has dispersed the energies or the power source of the querent. The interlacing circles have become entangled with the surrounding border of the card. The Five of Coins represents losses rather than gains which are both material and personal. The entangled pattern is symbolic of a disorderly situation. The card is traditionally linked to marriage problems due to financial worry or secret love-affairs outside of marriage.

The personal aspect shows a stubborn nature and a powerful self-will which can become irresponsible. The self-determination can, however, work constructively by forcing the issues and breaking a link or stranglehold that has become extremely negative. The losses incurred as a result can be related to job or profession and means a financial setback. A critical situation which requires a certain single-mindedness.

Dignified A question of priorities. Positive action will mean making a break and disregarding the consequences. The chaos or confusion can then be short-lived rather than extended.

Ill-dignified Financial problems create personal worry and strain. The health and vitality of the querent is under threat. Losses will occur that are extremely difficult to reverse.

Six of Coins

The six coins have formed a rose-shape hexagram with a spiralling centre of great force. The background of the card has also changed significantly. The green spirals have created four ornate crosses with the same spiralling centre. The energies of Earth are harmoniously united. The card is related to great wealth and power. The influence is liberal and just. It shows great prosperity and generosity.

It relates to present-day rather than future success. A successful conclusion, but not necessarily the end of the

matter. It also shows great accomplishment and personal prestige — the 'Midas touch' in business ventures. A positive and rewarding period in the life of the querent. Success has been reached through steady work and application, not an overnight success.

Dignified Prosperous business dealings. Fortunate friends and strong alliances. An exalted position in life which can be demanding but worthwhile.

Ill-dignified Paying the bills of others or being irresponsible with other people's money. A tremendous drain on the resources — heavy debts. Extravagant spending to create a false image.

Seven of Coins

The seven coins are grouped together to form a concentration of energies and shows a great deal of effort and labour. It is a significant aspect of the card, but the result is disappointing. Whilst the pattern has a definite shape, it has unequal proportions. The centre coin creates an illusion of being part of two separate designs that have the same trefoil pattern. It is symbolic of unfulfilled hopes and desires.

There is a very contradictory aspect to the card which relies on the symbolism of the neighbouring cards. Some success is possible, but it has a sense of great expectations rather than a definite financial return. The work may very well be seen as helping a friend, a personal commitment based on a non-profit making venture.

Dignified The reward of knowing a job is finished, and a personal account is settled. A methodical and practical application of skills which limits the outcome by being overly cautious.

Ill-dignified Loss of profit due to lack of sustained effort. Anxiety over bad investments. Not a time to lend money to friends. Disappointments and unfulfilled promises.

Eight of Coins

The dual energies are perfectly divided into two powerful symbols of the material world. The symbol of four is a perfect number of completion with the four elements of Earth in harmonious balance. The design of the card has a sense of perspective and intelligent reasoning. A strong base for building a future. The activity of the querent is concentrated on worthwhile ventures.

The creative skills are being fully utilized and directed. The beginning of a new cycle suggests the tide is turning in favour of the querent. A birth of a child may be imminent or a new skill is being perfected. The work may still be in the early stage of construction but shows great promise. The concentration of energies, however, can become too analytical or exacting in an effort to produce a 'masterpiece'. A dark young person is indicated.

Dignified Successful work behind the scenes. Positive preparation and planning. Involvement with community work or for the public generally. High expectations are justified.

Ill-dignified Some intrigue or mystery surrounds the nature of the work. The neighbouring cards show the extent of any negativity but generally this is a very productive card.

Nine of Coins

The nine coins have formed three sets of three. A complicated arrangement but a positive approach to the distribution of energy. The card has a powerful significance for good or bad. Whilst it symbolizes accomplishment and success, it can also become a source of bad faith or the distribution of wealth to the undeserving. It is, however, a card of material gain, often in the form of inheritance. The acquisition of wealth can promote envy and theft which are the negative aspects of the card.

The three series of three that make up the number nine have created a multiple force of energy. This energy is initially primed to create good luck and the increase of wealth. A positive card to draw if expecting a reward of any

 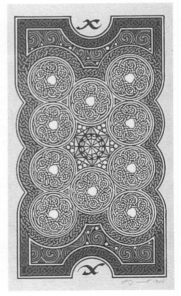

kind. It symbolizes above all else a certain self-reliance and a personal style. An impressive show of wealth rather than a superficial one.

Dignified Honours and material gains. The realization of self-worth has a deeper meaning or significance to the querent. An inheritance has more value than first imagined.

Ill-dignified Some deception or theft of money. Envy of others has marred an otherwise successful and rewarding experience. Money distributed in good faith has been used for illegal purposes.

Ten of Coins

The ten coins have again formed a rose-hexagram with a cubic centre of multiple facets. The outer four coins extend the boundaries but indicate a fixed position now reached. The whole design of the card signifies a completed success and suggests a retirement or a time to enjoy the profits. It is often a sign of old age and maturity.

A climactic cycle or period in the life of the querent is now related to family matters. The home becomes the centre of power and social activity. Grandchildren and dependants are a significant factor. Time to share the accumulated resources.

Dignified Positive use of power and position which can benefit others. Advice and encouragement to younger members of the family. The material wealth should be better invested.

Ill-dignified Some loss of investments, but not a serious setback. A lack of interest can indicate a slowing up generally. A fatality in the family that was expected after a long illness.

Page of Coins

The Page of Coins is holding the symbol of Coins, and the open book lying beside him symbolizes the scholarly application of learning. The Page represents a student or a young disciple. He is dressed in the green and brown colours of Earth. The stone cross in the background is a Celtic cross and indicates a time when all scholarly learning was administered by the Church. During that period, the sons of Celtic kings were educated in the monasteries, which were often located in remote places. But in pre-Christian times the Druids were tutors to the royal children.

The Celts valued scholarly studies and the arts. The Celtic race was once described by Marcus Cato, a Roman statesman and historian, as 'devoted to the art of war and the subtlety of speech'. It is a statement showing the distinct and intense character of the Celts. The card is also related to messages and messengers. It may relate to a contract or a commission; a careful examination of the facts which has been long awaited.

Dignified It shows a diligent youth. Favourable news of examinations concerning young people. Also a sign of courage and perseverance. Favourable news generally.

Ill-dignified A wasteful use of opportunity. An idle youth who causes great concern and disappointment. Important news is delayed.

Knight of Coins

The Knight of Coins rides slowly into the picture, head bowed in a thoughtful mood. He holds the reins loosely,

his direction is undecided. The shield has the symbol of Coins and his helmet, a golden plume. The noble brown horse represents the colour and energies of Earth. The violet flowers symbolize a spiritual mission about to begin as the Sun rises on the distant horizon. He is one of the Knights of the Round Table who eventually found the Holy Grail. His name is Sir Bors de Ganis, nephew of Sir Lancelot and the illegitimate son of King Arthur.

The character symbolized by this card has a meditative nature, with great energy solidly directed into a chosen goal, a lack of almost any emotion, but a steadfast and completely trustworthy character. Sir Bors was known for these qualities, also his vow of chastity. His imperturbable nature was a key to his success, a significant factor of the card. The negative qualities are stupidity, resentfulness and a slow anger which cannot be placated.

Dignified A competent character who supplies some discreet aid. A capable manager or agent who works hard behind the scenes to improve the finances of the querent.

Ill-dignified A stagnant situation where the querent cannot raise the capital to fund a worthwhile venture. An angry character who feels justified in attacking the querent.

Queen of Coins

The Queen of Coins is dressed in green, the fertile colour of Earth. She is holding a symbol of Coins to demonstrate her position of wealth and power. The golden pentacle on her dress is the magical symbol of Earth and shows the creative energies are fully realized. The Queen is the watery element of Earth, the most fertile and creative element of woman — the Mother. The character is more intuitive than intellectual. Whilst being an affectionate and caring mother, she is not inclined to spoil her children. She is practical and sensible, determined to make her children strong and self-sufficient.

Queen Margawse of Orkney was such a mother. Her four sons — Gawaine, Agravaine, Gaheris and Gareth — all became Knights of the Round Table. But the fatal flaw in her character was lust; Margawse was an unfaithful wife. She had also deliberately conceived an illegitimate child by King Arthur, her own brother, before he knew of their blood relationship. The child was Mordred, thus Margawse had produced four flowers of manhood and one poisonous viper.

Dignified A sensible woman; perhaps a keen business-woman who helps the querent with advice and some financial support. She is the ambitious type who can spot the strengths and weaknesses in others.

Ill-dignified A rather dull and foolish woman. Someone who lacks discretion and places the querent in a difficult position.

King of Coins

The King of Coins sits on a strange throne. The curious zoomorphic figure depicted in the design of the throne represents the Celtic expression of the mythical and semi-realistic. It signifies a form of power which again is non-intellectual and inclined to become engrossed with detail. The King is holding a long list or inventory of his possessions and estate. Here is the true materialist. Life itself can be exceedingly dull when the acquisition of wealth dominates.

King Lot of Orkney, the husband of Margawse, had opposed young King Arthur's claim to be the King of Britain. He was a rich and powerful king who laughed at Merlin's prediction of the Round Table and Arthur becoming the mightiest king of the realm. He saw only the young inexperienced boy; his lack of imagination was his weakness. Whilst he did not lack courage, he was inclined to jealousy. His type of character is found with the King of Coins.

Dignified A successful businessman, clever in financial matters but often insensitive to the arts, lacking a certain refinement. He will therefore only help the querent in matters of finance.

Ill-dignified Someone who is petty and interfering, who lacks vision and will try to spoil other people's hopes and dreams.

Bibliography and Recommended Reading

Bain, George, *Celtic Art: The Methods of Construction,* Constable, London, 1987.

Broadhurst, Paul, *Secret Shrines,* Paul Broadhurst, Limited Edition, Launceston, Cornwall, 1988.

Brown, Peter, *The Book of Kells,* Thames & Hudson, London, 1981.

Connolly, Eileen, *Tarot: A New Handbook for the Apprentice,* Newcastle Publishing Company, California, 1979; *Tarot: The Handbook for the Journeyman,* Newcastle Publishing Company, California, 1987. (Both books also available from The Aquarian Press.)

Cowie, Norma, *Tarot for Successful Living,* N.C. Publishing, White Rock, Canada, 1980.

Crowley, Aleister, *The Book of Thoth,* Samuel Weiser, Maine, 1988.

Cumont, Franz, *Astrology and Religion Among the Greeks and Romans,* Dover Publications, New York, 1960.

Davis, Courtney, *Celtic Art Source Book,* Blandford Press, London, 1988.

Dicta et Françoise, *Tarot de Marseilles,* Mercure de France, Paris, 1980.

Estens, John Locke, *The Paraclete and Mahdi,* John Sands Ltd, Sydney, 1912.

Graves, Robert, *The White Goddess,* Faber & Faber, London, 1971.

Gray, William G., *The Sangreal Tarot,* Samuel Weiser, Maine, 1988.

Hencken, H. O'Neill, *The Archaeology of Cornwall and Scilly*, Methuen & Co. Ltd, London, 1932.

Junjulas, Craig, *The Psychic Tarot*, Morgan & Morgan, New York, 1985.

Knight, Gareth, *A Practical Guide to Qabalistic Symbolism*, Helios Book Service (Publications), Cheltenham, 1972.

McLean, Adam, *The Four Fire Festivals*, Megalithic Research Publications, Edinburgh, 1979.

Malory, Sir Thomas, *Le Morte D'Arthur*, J. M. Dent & Sons Ltd, London, 1961.

Marteau, Paul, *Le Tarot de Marseilles*, Arts et Mètiers Graphiques, Neuchâtel, Switzerland, 1977.

Ouspensky, P.D., *The Symbolism of the Tarot*, Dover Publications, New York, 1976.

Rolleston, T.W., *Myths and Legends of the Celtic Race* (Second and Revised Edition), George G. Harrap & Co., London, 1917.

Spence, Lewis, *The Mysteries of Britain*, Rider & Co., London, 1931.

Thierens, A.E., *Astrology and the Tarot*, Newcastle Publishing Company, California, 1975.

Vogh, James, *Arachne Rising*, Granada Publishing, London, 1977.

Wang, Robert, *The Qabalistic Tarot*, Samuel Weiser, Maine, 1987.

Courtney Davis

Courtney Davis was born in South Wales in 1946, though most of his early life was spent living in London. His working life has been varied; he was a designer of wedding rings for one of the top jewellery companies, a signwriter, silkscreen printer and a furniture maker before embarking on his artistic career.

It was on a trip to Wales that he became interested in the Celts and their art, and gradually this art-form crept into his drawings, eventually taking over entirely. It was the success of the book called *Merlin the Immortal* in 1984 that made people aware of Courtney's talent, and it was followed a year later with *The Celtic Art of Courtney Davis*. Various projects have followed, including his own *The Celtic Art Sourcebook* in 1988, but the design and execution of *The Celtic Tarot* deck is his most ambitious project to date.

Courtney now has a large following in America, Canada and Europe and his unique work has been exhibited all over Britain and in Brittany and the USA. He has also designed a range of Celtic jewellery, posters and cards which can be obtained through the CELTIA catalogue. This can be obtained by writing (with a stamped addressed envelope) to: CELTIA, Woodbine Cottage, Newcause, Buckfastleigh, South Devon TQ11 0AZ.